Fifth Edition

SPANISH VERB DRILLS

by
Vivienne Bey

in collaboration with
Beatrice Concheff and Jean Yates

New York   Chicago   San Francisco   Lisbon   London   Madrid   Mexico City
Milan   New Delhi   San Juan   Seoul   Singapore   Sydney   Toronto

4 5 6 7 8 9 0   LHS   22 21 20 19

ISBN: 978-1-260-01066-4
MHID: 1-260-01066-X

e-ISBN: 978-1-260-01067-1
e-MHID: 0-1-260-01067-8

McGraw-Hill Education books are available at special quantity discounts to use as premiums and sales promotions or for use in corporate training programs. To contact a representative, please visit the Contact Us pages at www.mhprofessional.com.

McGraw-Hill Education Language Lab App

Review quizzes, flash cards, and a digital glossary are all available to support your study of this book. Go to www.mhlanguagelab.com to access the online version of the application, or to locate links to the mobile app for iOS and Android devices. More details about the features of the app are available on the inside front cover.

Also in this series
Vallecillos: *Spanish Grammar Drills*
Gordon & Stillman: *Spanish Vocabulary Drills*

Contents

Introduction

Spanish Verb Drills is designed to help learners develop mastery of the Spanish verb system. Created to supplement the oral and written verb practice offered by standard Spanish-language textbooks, it provides students at all levéis with the drill and review needed to grasp the tenses and conjugations of Spanish verbs.

Models at the beginning of each unit establish the patterns to be reinforced in the *Para practicar* drills, the *Aplicación* exercises, and the Mastery Tests. In addition, the four-part *Repaso general* allows students to test themselves for overall control of the Spanish verb system.

Combining the features of a workbook, textbook, and self-study manual, *Spanish Verb Drills* clearly and systematically explains the workings of the Spanish verb system, while providing numerous and varied exercises for thorough practice of each point covered. This latest edition has been enhanced by more detailed coverage of the imperative. It is also supported by the McGraw-Hill Education Language Lab app, which contains flashcards for all verbs lists in the book and additional quizzes for study on-the-go.

Covering verb tenses ranging from the present indicative to the imperfect subjunctive and offering detailed treatment of stem-changing verbs, orthographic-changing verbs, and irregular verbs, *Spanish Verb Drills* will serve as an invaluable study aid to all those wishing to perfect their knowledge of Spanish verbs. Equally suitable in a Spanish-language course or for self-study, this book effectively clarifies the complexities of this crucial area of Spanish-language study.

1 Regular Verbs
Present

Spanish verbs are classified into three classes, or *conjugations*, according to the final letters of their infinitives. The present tense of regular verbs is formed by adding the personal endings to the *stem*, which is determined by dropping the *-ar*, *-er*, or *-ir* of the infinitive.

	1 *habl*ar to speak		*2* *com*er to eat		*3* *part*ir to leave
yo	habl *o* I speak, am speaking, do speak	com *o* I eat, etc.		part *o* I leave, etc.	
tú	habl *as* you speak, etc.	com *es* you eat, etc.		part *es* you leave, etc.	
Ud.	habl *a* you speak, etc.	com *e* you eat, etc.		part *e* you leave, etc.	
él(ella)	habl *a* he(she) speaks, etc.	com *e* he(she) eats, etc.		part *e* he(she) leaves, etc.	
nosotros	habl *amos* we speak, etc.	com *emos* we eat, etc.		part *imos* we leave, etc.	
vosotros	habl *áis* you speak, etc.	com *éis* you eat, etc.		part *ís* you leave, etc.	
Uds.	habl *an* you speak, etc.	com *en* you eat, etc.		part *en* you leave, etc.	
ellos (ellas)	habl *an* they speak, etc.	com *en* they eat, etc.		part *en* they leave, etc.	

1. Spanish has no equivalent for the English *am* (is, are) or *do* (does) in the present tense. The single verb *hablo* means *I am speaking*, *I do speak*, or *I speak*.

2. The pronoun subject of the Spanish verb is expressed by the ending of the verb. The verb must show this personal ending, even if a subject pronoun or noun is already present in the sentence. The subject pronouns (*yo*, etc.) are seldom used in actual practice, except for *Ud*. and *Uds*. Remember that there are two singular and two plural forms of the second person (you), for informal and formal use. The *tú* and *vosotros* forms of the verb may not be used with the subjects *Ud*. and *Uds*., or vice versa.

3. The Spanish word *si*, translated as *if*, indicates that what follows is probably true or will probably happen, and is followed by a present tense verb.
   If Jorge eats meat, …   *si Jorge come carne, …*
   If Jorge doesn't eat meat, …   *si Jorge no come carne, …*
   If Susana arrives on time, …   *si Susana llega a tiempo, …*
   If Susana doesn't arrive on time, …   *si Susana no llega a tiempo, …*

Negative: All Spanish verbs form the negative by placing *no* before the verb.
   He eats *come*;   he does not eat *no come*.

Interrogative: All Spanish verbs in the interrogative are identical to the affirmative.
   He eats *come*;   does he eat? ¿*come*?
   Spanish verbs in the negative-interrogative are identical to the negative.
   He does not eat *no come*;   doesn't he eat? ¿*no come*?

Para practicar

All regular verbs with infinitives ending in *-ar* form the present like *hablar*. Write the present tense of (1) *acabar* to finish, and (2) *tomar* to take.

(1) **acabar** yo _ACAbo_

tú _ACAbas_

Ud. _CcAb_

él _____

nosotros _____

vosotros _____

Uds. _____

ellos _____

(2) **tomar** yo _____

tú _____

Ud. _____

ella _____

nosotros _____

vosotros _____

Uds. _____

ellos _____

All regular verbs with infinitives in *-er* form the present like *comer*. Write the present tense of (1) *vender* to sell, and (2) *beber* to drink.

(1) **vender** yo _____

tú _____

Ud. _____

él _____

nosotros _____

vosotros _____

Uds. _____

ellos _____

(2) **beber** yo _____

tú _____

Ud. _____

él _____

nosotros _____

vosotros _____

Uds. _____

ellos _____

All regular verbs with infinitives in *-ir* form the present like *partir*. Write the present tense of
(1) *vivir*   to live, and (2) *recibir*   to receive.

(1) **vivir**	yo _____	(2) **recibir**	yo _____
	tú _____		tú _____
	Ud. _____		Ud. _____
	él _____		él _____
	nosotros _____		nosotros _____
	vosotros _____		vosotros _____
	Uds. _____		Uds. _____
	ellos _____		ellos _____

Change the infinitives below into the correct form of the present, according to the subject indicated:

yo

estudiar	comprender	temer	necesitar	partir	enseñar
_____	_____	_____	_____	_____	_____

vender

_____

tú

hablar	asistir	abrir	beber	preguntar	tomar
_____	_____	_____	_____	_____	_____

escuchar

_____

4

Ud.

contestar	abrir	aprender	entrar	leer	vivir
_____	_____	_____	_____	_____	_____

comer

_____

Juan (what person?)

escribir	estudiar	acabar	temer	partir	comprender
_____	_____	_____	_____	_____	_____

vender

_____

nosotros

aprender	asistir	tomar	escuchar	hablar	vivir
_____	_____	_____	_____	_____	_____

temer

_____

vosotros

hablar	asistir	beber	leer	tomar	llevar
_____	_____	_____	_____	_____	_____

enseñar

_____

Uds.

comer	escribir	necesitar	entrar	acabar	leer
_____	_____	_____	_____	_____	_____

vivir

_____

María y Juan (what person?)

temer	llevar	estudiar	preguntar	contestar	comprender
_____	_____	_____	_____	_____	_____

partir

_____

Aplicación

A. Write the verb forms in the person indicated by the pronoun:

1. nosotros (tomar) _____

2. él (aprender) _____

3. ellos (vender) _____

4. yo (asistir) _____

5. tú (contestar) _____

6. Ud. (beber) _____

7. nosotras (abrir) _____

8. ella (necesitar) _____

9. vosotros (tomar) _____

10. ella (leer) _____

11. yo (aprender) _____

12. nosotros (temer) _____

13. vosotros (recibir) _____

14. ellos (escribir) _____

15. ella (abrir) _____

16. nosotros (enseñar) _____

17. yo (contestar) _____

18. nosotros (estudiar) _____

19. yo (abrir) _____

20. ella (tomar) _____

21. Ud. (preguntar) _____

22. ellas (leer) _____

23. ellos (recibir) _____

24. tú (temer) _____

25. nosotras (leer) _____

B. Change each verb form to the corresponding person of the plural, and translate the plural verb into English:

1. escribo _____

_____

2. él contesta _____

_____

3. vivo _____

_____

4. Ud. necesita _____

_____

5. él bebe _____

_____

6. aprendes _____

_____

7. él vende _____

_____

8. asisto _____

_____

9. Ud. enseña _____

_____

10. abres _____

_____

11. Ud. comprende _____

_____

12. ella escucha _____

_____

13. temes _____

_____

14. ella pregunta _____

_____

15. Ud. lee _____

_____

16. tomo _____

_____

17. recibo _____

_____

18. él estudia _____

_____

19. necesito _____

_____

20. escribes _____

_____

Mastery Test

estudiar to study	*trabajar* to work	*esconder* to hide
necesitar to need	*comprender* to understand	*vivir* to live
contestar to answer	*beber* to drink	*recibir* to receive
preguntar to ask	*vender* to sell	*asistir* to attend
enseñar to teach	*aprender* to learn	*abrir* to open
escuchar to listen	*temer* to fear	*escribir* to write
tomar to take	*leer* to read	*unir* to join, unite
entrar to enter	*creer* to believe	

Translate the following, using the above list of infinitives:

1. we answer _____

2. you (pl., fam.) sell _____

3. he is asking _____

4. if they do sell _____

5. we do not need _____

6. if we study _____

7. I am learning _____

8. do they listen? _____

9. he is not reading _____

10. you (s., for.) are not entering _____

11. if we work _____

12. do you write? _____

13. if they do ask _____

14. if you (pl., for.) are taking _____

15. I sell _____

16. she does not work _____

17. they do not believe _____

18. they hide _____

19. if he writes _____

20. do you fear? _____

21. we are living _____

22. he teaches _____

23. she fears _____

24. you (pl., fam.) receive _____

25. he is opening _____

26. if they do not take _____

27. if we attend _____

28. is he selling? _____

29. I study _____

30. I believe _____

31. they unite _____

32. they are not opening _____

33. if you teach _____

34. he attends _____

35. we ask _____

36. do you (pl., for.) learn? _____

37. if she drinks _____

38. are you (s., fam.) studying? _____

39. you (s., for.) live _____

40. they enter _____

2 Imperfect

The imperfect is formed by adding the appropriate endings to the stem.

	1 hablar	*2* comer	*3* partir
yo	habl *aba* I was speaking,	com *ía* I was eating,	part *ía* I was leaving,
tú	habl *abas* used to speak	com *ías* used to eat	part *ías* used to leave
Ud.	habl *aba*	com *ía*	part *ía*
él(ella)	habl *aba*	com *ía*	part *ía*
nosotros	habl *ábamos*	com *íamos*	part *íamos*
vosotros	habl *abais*	com *íais*	part *íais*
Uds.	habl *aban*	com *ían*	part *ían*
ellos	habl *aban*	com *ían*	part *ían*

All forms of the imperfect of *-er* and *-ir* verbs must have a written accent. Because first- and third-person singular forms are identical, context determines the subject for them.

Note: The imperfect has three clearly separate meanings in English:

1. It describes the way things were, and the things people did, during a specific period of time in the past:
   I (always) ate lunch at school.
   I would (always) eat lunch at school. *Yo comía en la escuela.*
   I used to (always) eat lunch at school.
   I (always) ate lunch at school.

2. It sets the scene for a narration in the past:
   It was a dark night. *Era una noche oscura.*
   It was raining. *Llovía.*
   We were lost. *Estábamos perdidos.*

3. It depicts action that was in progress in the past:
   We were walking home. *Caminábamos a casa.*
   My friend was talking. *Mi amigo hablaba.*
   I was thinking about my dad. *Estaba pensando en mi papá.*

Para practicar

Write the form of the imperfect that corresponds to the subject indicated:

yo

tomar	meter	vivir	comprar	sentir	viajar
_____	_____	_____	_____	_____	_____

correr

_____

tú

aprender	subir	pasar	guardar	coser	esperar
_____	_____	_____	_____	_____	_____

acabar

_____

Ud.

tocar	amar	saber	jugar	viajar	comprender
_____	_____	_____	_____	_____	_____

escribir

_____

María

echar	preparar	leer	vivir	abrir	correr
_____	_____	_____	_____	_____	_____

trabajar

_____

nosotros

estudiar	vender	subir	comprender	abrir	preparar
_____	_____	_____	_____	_____	_____

tomar

_____

vosotros

escribir	trabajar	comer	beber	recibir	comprar
_____	_____	_____	_____	_____	_____

llevar

_____

Juan y Ud. (What person?)

pasar	caminar	responder	subir	hablar	abrir
_____	_____	_____	_____	_____	_____

sacar

_____

ellos

acabar	salir	contestar	vivir	guardar	correr
_____	_____	_____	_____	_____	_____

viajar

_____

Aplicación

A. Write the imperfect form in the person indicated by the subject:

1. él (hablar) _____

2. Elena y yo (vivir) _____

3. ella (saber) _____

4. Uds. (conocer) _____

5. los niños (pedir) _____

6. nosotros (correr) _____

7. tú (partir) _____

8. yo (pasar) _____

9. vosotros (esperar) _____

10. Uds. (acabar) _____

11. Ud. (caminar) _____

12. él (comprender) _____

13. Juan y Pedro (tomar) _____

14. yo (escribir) _____

B. Change to imperfect and translate the new form into one of its meanings in English:

1. contestamos _____

2. vendes _____

3. él pregunta _____

4. aprendo _____

5. ellos escuchan _____

6. Ud. escribe _____

7. ellos aprenden _____

8. Ud. estudia _____

9. vivimos _____

10. él teme _____

11. él abre _____

12. ellos enseñan _____

13. él asiste _____

14. tomamos _____

15. Ud. (amar) _____

16. vosotros (conocer) _____

17. tú (beber) _____

18. nosotros (comprar) _____

19. ellos (subir) _____

20. yo (correr) _____

21. ella (responder) _____

22. tú (guardar) _____

23. Ud. (aprender) _____

24. Juan y él (llevar) _____

25. vosotros (pasar) _____

15. leo _____

16. Uds. beben _____

17. temo _____

18. ellos reciben _____

19. necesito _____

20. Uds. viven _____

21. abrimos _____

22. contestáis _____

23. tomas _____

24. él bebe _____

25. abrís _____

Mastery Test

Write the Spanish that corresponds to the English verb forms, selecting the correct verb from the list on page 6.

1. they used to live _____

2. we were working _____

3. you (s., fam.) were not selling _____

_____

4. we used to live _____

5. they did not need _____

6. you (s., for.) were learning _____

_____

7. he used to believe _____

8. you (pl., fam.) were asking _____

_____

9. I used to fear _____

10. did you (s., fam.) understand? _____

_____

11. she was teaching _____

12. you (pl., for.) used to take _____

_____

13. we were not listening _____

_____

14. he used to sell _____

15. you (pl., for.) were opening _____

_____

16. did they always receive …? _____

17. we were attending _____

18. you (s., fam.) used to study _____

_____

19. he was reading _____

20. they were living _____

21. you (pl., for.) were not hiding _____

_____

22. I used to receive _____

23. they did not understand _____

_____

24. I was eating _____

25. you (s., for.) used to sell _____

_____

26. you (s., fam.) were not taking _____

_____

27. they were listening _____

28. was he attending? _____

29. you (pl., fam.) used to need _____

_____

30. she was answering _____

_____

3 Preterit

The preterit is formed in regular verbs by adding the preterit endings to the stem.

	1	*2*	*3*
	hablar	**comer**	**partir**
yo	habl *é* I spoke, I did speak	com *í* I ate,	part *í* I left, did
tú	habl *aste* you spoke, etc.	com *iste* did eat	part *iste* leave
Ud.	habl *ó*	com *ió*	part *ió*
él(ella)	habl *ó*	com *ió*	part *ió*
nosotros	habl *amos*	com *imos*	part *imos*
vosotros	habl *asteis*	com *isteis*	part *isteis*
Uds.	habl *aron*	com *ieron*	part *ieron*
ellos	habl *aron*	com *ieron*	part *ieron*

Note: The preterit is translated as the English past tense:

I spoke/I did speak   *Hablé*
I didn't speak   *No hablé*
Did I speak?   *¿Hablé?*

In this manual *I spoke* will be translated with the preterit as will *I did speak*. In negative or interrogative verbs, *I did not....* or *did I....* may indicate either imperfect or preterit.

Para practicar

Write the preterit of each verb that corresponds to the subject indicated:

yo

viajar	trabajar	estudiar	comer	vender	insistir
_____	_____	_____	_____	_____	_____

recibir

_____

tú

unir	acabar	comprar	romper	correr	abrir
_____	_____	_____	_____	_____	_____

tomar

_____

Ud.

comer	asistir	echar	preparar	subir	pasar
_____	_____	_____	_____	_____	_____

trabajar

_____

Pepe

viajar	hablar	aprender	resistir	llamar	responder
_____	_____	_____	_____	_____	_____

echar

_____

nosotros

trabajar	comprar	amar	vender	beber	correr
_____	_____	_____	_____	_____	_____

vivir

_____

tú y él

estudiar	comer	abrir	tomar	viajar	subir
_____	_____	_____	_____	_____	_____

pasar

_____

Uds.

trabajar	comprar	hablar	aprender	temer	escribir
_____	_____	_____	_____	_____	_____

viajar

_____

ellos

guardar	comprender	asistir	abrir	pasar	echar
_____	_____	_____	_____	_____	_____

beber

_____

Aplicación

A. Write the following infinitives in the preterit and in the person indicated by the subject.

1. yo (llevar) _____
2. nosotros (abrir) _____
3. tú (llegar) _____
4. Pepe y Juan (comer) _____
5. ella (beber) _____
6. tú y él (meter) _____
7. María y Elena (viajar) _____
8. Ud. (vivir) _____
9. mis amigos (pasar) _____
10. Uds. (vender) _____
11. yo (abrir) _____
12. Pablo (asistir) _____
13. ellos (recibir) _____
14. nosotras (tomar) _____
15. vosotros (temer) _____
16. ella (abrir) _____
17. Juan y él (escribir) _____
18. Uds. (necesitar) _____

B. Write (1) the preterit and (2) the imperfect of each verb given in the present.

1. tomamos _____
2. enseñan _____
3. Ud. contesta _____
4. reciben _____
5. aprende _____
6. asisto _____
7. tememos _____
8. venden _____
9. aprendo _____
10. contesto _____
11. Uds. toman _____
12. abre _____
13. necesita _____
14. recibes _____
15. trabaja _____
16. echan _____
17. suben _____
18. comprendo _____

16

A. Write the following infinitives in the preterit and in the person indicated by the subject. (*continued*)

19. tú (vender) _____

20. nosotros (beber) _____

21. ellos (aprender) _____

22. yo (tomar) _____

23. ella (estudiar) _____

24. Ud. (beber) _____

25. yo (recibir) _____

B. Write (1) the preterit and (2) the imperfect of each verb given in the present. (*continued*)

19. corre _____

20. trabajo _____

21. Ud. prepara _____

22. guardan _____

23. pasamos _____

24. viajo _____

25. echas _____

Mastery Test

Write in the preterit, using infinitives on page 6.

1. we answered _____

2. they sold _____

3. I learned _____

4. did you (s., fam.) listen? _____

_____

5. she did not ask _____

6. you (s., for.) hid _____

7. we took _____

8. they did not drink _____

9. we attended _____

10. I did teach _____

11. you (s., fam.) asked _____

12. they worked _____

13. you (pl., for.) joined _____

14. I lived _____

15. you (pl., fam.) answered _____

_____

16. you (pl., for.) did write _____

_____

17. she understood _____

18. they did not learn _____

19. we wrote _____

20. did he study? _____

21. you (s., fam.) sold _____

22. he taught _____

23. he attended _____

24. I sold _____

25. you (pl., fam.) did live _____

_____

26. they received _____

27. I attended _____

28. they asked _____

29. we drank _____

30. you (s., for.) studied _____

31. I did not answer _____

32. did you (pl., for.) open? _____

_____

33. they did not understand _____

_____

34. you (s., fam.) did not need _____

_____

35. we sold _____

36. did you (s., for.) take? _____

_____

37. we did not receive _____

38. she feared _____

39. I wrote _____

40. did you (pl., fam.) ask? _____

Repaso (Present, imperfect, preterit)

Write in Spanish, using the infinitives below and on page 6.

echar	to throw	*preparar*	to prepare
viajar	to travel	*responder*	to reply, respond
pasar	to pass, spend	*correr*	to run
guardar	to keep	*subir*	to go up

1. they used to live _____

2. I was opening _____

3. they did work _____

4. we were going up _____

5. I understand _____

6. they did not take _____

7. he was running _____

8. they answered _____

9. I work _____

10. you (s., fam.) prepared _____
_____

11. you (pl., for.) used to study _____
_____

12. they keep _____

13. we were spending _____

14. I traveled _____

15. you (s., for.) need _____

16. I was not living _____

17. you (pl., for.) used to open _____
_____

18. he (always) used to write _____

19. I go up _____

20. he did understand _____

21. I was writing _____

22. you (s., fam.) respond _____

23. we understood _____

24. you (pl., fam.) did not learn _____
_____

25. they are preparing _____

26. we learn _____

27. we ran _____

28. you (pl., for.) were spending _____
_____

29. they did work _____

30. we attend _____

31. we were not writing _____

32. I threw _____

33. we were studying _____

34. I worked _____

35. we were living _____

36. we kept _____

37. you (s., fam.) understood _____
_____

38. they attended _____

39. we (always) used to sell _____

40. I am spending _____

41. I lived _____

42. you (s., fam.) fear _____

43. she listened _____

44. you (pl., fam.) did not keep _____
_____

45. he is drinking _____

46. they would (always) keep _____

47. he left _____

48. you (s., for.) feared _____

49. we went up _____

50. I do not answer _____

4 Future

The future of regular verbs is formed by adding the future endings to the full infinitive or, in some irregular verbs, to a modified form of the infinitive.

	1 **hablar**	*2* **comer**	*3* **partir**
yo	hablar *é* I will speak	comer *é* I will eat	partir *é* I will leave
tú	hablar *ás*	comer *ás*	partir *ás*
Ud.	hablar *á*	comer *á*	partir *á*
él(ella)	hablar *á*	comer *á*	partir *á*
nosotros	hablar *emos*	comer *emos*	partir *emos*
vosotros	hablar *éis*	comer *éis*	partir *éis*
Uds.	hablar *án*	comer *án*	partir *án*
ellos	hablar *án*	comer *án*	partir *án*

Future endings are the same for all three conjugations of verbs. All forms of the future except the first-person plural have a written accent.

Note: The future usually translates as "will" in English. It indicates what one predicts for a future too distant or uncertain to plan.

I will travel to the moon.   *Viajaré a la luna.*
They will (probably) arrive late.   *Llegarán tarde.*

Para practicar

Write the future form of each verb that corresponds to the subject indicated:

yo

comprar	hablar	leer	vivir	sentir	ser
_____	_____	_____	_____	_____	_____

asistir

_____

tú

estudiar	encontrar	correr	tomar	vender	conocer
_____	_____	_____	_____	_____	_____

partir

_____

Ud.

enseñar	perder	dormir	aprender	recibir	abrir
_____	_____	_____	_____	_____	_____

necesitar

_____

Juan

dudar	creer	amar	escribir	guardar	correr
_____	_____	_____	_____	_____	_____

subir

_____

nosotros

contestar	temer	preguntar	subir	viajar	aprender
_____	_____	_____	_____	_____	_____

vivir

_____

vosotros

preparar	echar	contestar	trabajar	viajar	responder
_____	_____	_____	_____	_____	_____

amar

_____

Uds.

comprar	leer	sentir	recibir	decidir	andar
_____	_____	_____	_____	_____	_____

pasar

_____

22

los niños

preparar   aprender   echar   viajar   contestar   correr

_____   _____   _____   _____   _____   _____

marchar

_____

Aplicación

A. Change the infinitive to correspond to the person indicated by the subject. Make all verbs future.

1. él (hablar) _____

2. nosotros (estar) _____

3. ella (ser) _____

4. Uds. (encontrar) _____

5. Juan (leer) _____

6. yo (dudar) _____

7. nosotros (perder) _____

8. tú (enseñar) _____

9. vosotros (dormir) _____

10. Ud. (andar) _____

11. tú (decidir) _____

12. yo (comprar) _____

13. él (vivir) _____

14. Ud. (sentir) _____

15. María (beber) _____

16. vosotros (estudiar) _____

17. él (abrir) _____

18. tú (vender) _____

19. ellos (escuchar) _____

20. Uds. (aprender) _____

21. ella (necesitar) _____

22. Ud. (contestar) _____

23. nosotras (temer) _____

24. yo (tomar) _____

25. tú (recibir) _____

B. Change all verbs to future and translate new forms into English.

1. (ellos) vivían _____

_____

2. abrí _____

_____

3. subimos _____

_____

4. comprendías _____

_____

5. aprendimos _____

_____

6. (ellos) trabajaron _____

_____

7. Ud. corría _____

_____

8. (ellas) contestaban _____

_____

9. trabajé _____

_____

10. preparabais _____

_____

11. pasábamos _____

_____

12. viajo _____

_____

13. echabas _____

_____

14. partí _____

_____

15. abríais _____

_____

16. Uds. escribían _____

_____

17. subí _____

_____

18. (ella) comprendió _____

_____

19. corrimos _____

_____

20. Ud. contestó _____

_____

21. tomamos _____

_____

22. (ellos) enseñaron _____

_____

23. acababas _____

_____

24. (él) trabajaba _____

_____

25. escribí _____

_____

24

Mastery Test

Write in Spanish in the tense indicated by the English, using the infinitives below.

admirar to admire   *llamar* to call   *discutir* to discuss   *ofender* to offend
adornar to adorn   *limpiar* to clean   *insistir* to insist   *emprender* to undertake
molestar to bother   *cubrir* to cover   *decidir* to decide

1. you (s., fam.) will adorn _____

_____

2. I was admiring _____

3. you (pl., fam.) will offend _____

_____

4. he bothers _____

5. you (pl., for.) will discuss _____

_____

6. I insisted _____

7. he will discuss _____

8. we will undertake _____

9. they will clean _____

10. you (pl., for.) are calling _____

_____

11. I will admire _____

12. he adorned _____

13. you (s., fam.) bother _____

_____

14. I will discuss _____

15. they insisted _____

16. they were covering _____

17. we will cover _____

18. we admired _____

19. you (pl., for.) undertook _____

_____

20. we insist _____

21. they discussed _____

22. we will clean _____

23. he was cleaning _____

24. I decided _____

25. she is calling _____

26. we were offending _____

27. we will call _____

28. you (s., for.) did discuss _____

_____

29. we will not admire _____

30. they do not call _____

31. you (pl., fam.) are deciding _____

_____

32. I covered _____

33. you (s., for.) will not discuss _____

_____

34. we will not decide _____

35. will you (s., fam.) clean? _____

_____

36. you (pl., fam.) will not insist _____

_____

37. they will cover _____

38. you (pl., for.) cleaned _____

_____

39. we were insisting _____

40. he offended _____

5 Conditional

The conditional is formed by adding the conditional endings to the full infinitive or, in some irregular verbs, to a modified form of the infinitive.

	1		*2*		*3*	
	hablar		**comer**		**partir**	
yo	hablar *ía*	I should,	comer *ía*	I should,	partir *ía*	I should,
tú	hablar *ías*	would speak,	comer *ías*	would eat	partir *ías*	would
Ud.	hablar *ía*	etc.	comer *ía*		partir *ía*	leave
él(ella)	hablar *ía*		comer *ía*		partir *ía*	
nosotros	hablar *íamos*		comer *íamos*		partir *íamos*	
vosotros	hablar *íais*		comer *íais*		partir *íais*	
Uds.	hablar *ían*		comer *ían*		partir *ían*	
ellos	hablar *ían*		comer *ían*		partir *ían*	

All conditional forms must have a written accent.

Note: The conditional translates as *would* in English, and often follows an "*if* + imperfect subjunctive" clause. (See pp. 46–48.)

Para practicar

Write the conditional form that corresponds to the subject indicated:

yo

admirar	decidir	trabajar	vivir	beber	abrir
_____	_____	_____	_____	_____	_____

morir

_____

tú

adornar	ofender	responder	estudiar	vender	escribir
_____	_____	_____	_____	_____	_____

sentir

_____

Ud.

molestar	emprender	correr	necesitar	aprender	llevar
————————	————————	————————	————————	————————	————————

partir

————————

él

llamar	echar	aprender	contestar	temer	sacar
————————	————————	————————	————————	————————	————————

hablar

————————

Luisa y yo

limpiar	viajar	comprender	preguntar	leer	tocar
————————	————————	————————	————————	————————	————————

comer

————————

tú y Juan

cubrir	pasar	subir	enseñar	creer	conocer
————————	————————	————————	————————	————————	————————

meter

————————

Uds.

discutir	guardar	abrir	escuchar	recibir	traer
————————	————————	————————	————————	————————	————————

pedir

————————

ellas

insistir	preparar	escribir	tomar	asistir	dormir
_____	_____	_____	_____	_____	_____

rogar

_____

Aplicación

A. Change the infinitives to the conditional, according to the person of the subject.

1. ellas (admirar) _____

2. Ud. (discutir) _____

3. tú (cubrir) _____

4. yo (limpiar) _____

5. tú y Juan (vender) _____

6. él (preguntar) _____

7. él y ella (vender) _____

8. nosotros (estudiar) _____

9. mi amigo y yo (vivir) _____

10. María (temer) _____

11. Pepe (abrir) _____

12. ellas (tomar) _____

13. nosotras (escribir) _____

14. María y él (contestar) _____

_____

15. Uds. (temer) _____

B. a) Change from the future to the conditional and translate.

1. contestaremos _____

2. aprenderé _____

3. (ellos) escucharán _____

4. (él) leerá _____

5. esconderemos _____

6. escribiréis _____

7. (Uds.) estudiarán _____

8. venderé _____

9. (ella) enseñará _____

10. (ellas) comprenderán _____

b) Change from the imperfect to the conditional and translate.

1. (Uds.) vivían _____

2. (él) abría _____

3. (ellos) trabajaban _____

4. subíamos _____

16. tú (llevar) _____

17. yo (beber) _____

18. Ud. (aprender) _____

19. él (echar) _____

20. ellos (viajar) _____

21. vosotros (necesitar) _____

22. Uds. (escuchar) _____

23. nosotras (enseñar) _____

24. ellas (asistir) _____

25. tú (recibir) _____

5. (él) comprendía _____

6. aprendíais _____

7. (él) corría _____

8. preparabas _____

9. guardábamos _____

10. (ella) viajaba _____

Mastery Test

Write in Spanish to correspond to the English tense and person.

1. you (s., fam.) will decide _____

_____

2. I should bother _____

3. you (s., for.) were adorning _____

_____

4. would he offend? _____

5. I insisted _____

6. we would discuss _____

7. they admired _____

8. he would not adorn _____

9. I will not offend _____

10. they were offending _____

11. would she clean? _____

12. they undertake _____

13. they would admire _____

14. I will clean _____

15. you (pl., for.) would bother _____

_____

16. we will not cover _____

17. he covers _____

18. they would decide _____

19. will you (s., fam.) admire? _____

_____

20. we admired _____

21. they were insisting _____

22. I would not insist _____

23. you (pl., for.) cleaned _____

_____

24. she would decide _____

25. you (s., fam.) will insist _____

_____

26. would they call? _____

27. you (pl., fam.) would cover _____

_____

28. we will bother _____

29. they would not offend _____

_____

30. will I decide? _____

6 Progressive Tenses

Progressive tenses are compound tenses consisting of the appropriate tenses of *estar* and the present participle.

Present Participle: The present participle is formed by adding the ending *-ando* or *-iendo* to the infinitive stem.

1	*2*	*3*
hablar	**comer**	**partir**
habl *ando* speaking	com *iendo* eating	part *iendo* leaving

Note: The present participle has only one form; it does not distinguish person or number.

Estar   to be (in a state or condition)   (see page 112 for complete verb).

Present Progressive: The present progressive is formed with the present tense of *estar* plus the present participle. It is used to describe action thought of as in *progress*.

yo	*estoy*	*hablando, comiendo, partiendo*	I am (in the act of) speaking, eating,
tú	*estás*	hab*lando*, com*iendo*, part*iendo*	leaving
Ud.	*está*	hab*lando*, com*iendo*, part*iendo*	you are speaking, eating, leaving.
él(ella)	*está*	hab*lando*, com*iendo*, part*iendo*	
nosotros	*estamos*	hab*lando*, com*iendo*, part*iendo*	
vosotros	*estáis*	hab*lando*, com*iendo*, part*iendo*	
Uds.	*están*	hab*lando*, com*iendo*, part*iendo*	
ellos	*están*	hab*lando*, com*iendo*, part*iendo*	

Past Progressive: The past progressive is formed with the imperfect tense of *estar* plus the present participle. It describes action which *was* in progress at a given moment in the past.

yo	*estaba*	hab*lando*, com*iendo*, part*iendo*	I was (in the act of) speaking, eating,
tú	*estabas*	hab*lando*, com*iendo*, part*iendo*	leaving
Ud.	*estaba*	hab*lando*, com*iendo*, part*iendo*	you were speaking, etc.
él(ella)	*estaba*	hab*lando*, com*iendo*, part*iendo*	
nosotros	*estábamos*	hab*lando*, com*iendo*, part*iendo*	
vosotros	*estabais*	hab*lando*, com*iendo*, part*iendo*	
Uds.	*estaban*	hab*lando*, com*iendo*, part*iendo*	
ellos	*estaban*	hab*lando*, com*iendo*, part*iendo*	

Note: The present and past progressive tenses are used to express present or past (imperfect) action when that action is thought of as *continuing* or *in progress*. They are thus a more vivid, dramatic substitute for the present and imperfect, respectively. The *estar* verb indicates the person and number of the subject; the participle *always* remains the same.

Para practicar

Write the present participles of the following infinitives:

admirar	adornar	subir	cubrir	acabar	correr
_____	_____	_____	_____	_____	_____

responder	tomar	sacar	decidir	dar
_____	_____	_____	_____	_____

Write the present progressive form that corresponds to the subject:

yo

abrir	llevar	perder	buscar	estudiar	beber
_____	_____	_____	_____	_____	_____

tú

vivir	aprender	tomar	escribir	trabajar	enseñar
_____	_____	_____	_____	_____	_____

Uds.

vender	abrir	contestar	asistir	escuchar	entrar
_____	_____	_____	_____	_____	_____

nosotros

recibir	echar	admirar	pasar	responder	correr
_____	_____	_____	_____	_____	_____

Aplicación

A. Write the past progressive form for the subject indicated.

1. Juan (llevar) _____

2. tú (estudiar) _____

3. vosotros (trabajar) _____

B. Change the present and imperfect verbs so that they express action in progress, keeping the original subject.

1. reciben _____

2. trabajábamos _____

3. abrís _____

4. Pepe y yo (subir) _____

5. ellas (correr) _____

6. mi amigo (escuchar) _____

_____

7. los niños (jugar) _____

8. nosotros (escribir) _____

9. tú (comer) _____

10. ella (partir) _____

11. ella y yo (tomar) _____

12. él y ella (acabar) _____

13. yo (responder) _____

14. ellos (decidir) _____

15. él (cubrir) _____

4. preguntabais _____

5. no escuchaba _____

6. vivimos _____

7. bebe _____

8. Uds. asistían _____

9. vendes _____

10. Ud. no tomaba _____

11. enseñaba _____

12. contestáis _____

13. Ud. estudia _____

14. no comía _____

15. aprendo _____

Mastery Test

Express each English verb two ways:

1. I was admiring _____ _____

2. you (s., fam.) are deciding _____ _____

3. he was cleaning _____ _____

4. they were insisting _____ _____

5. if they are not preparing _____ _____

6. you (s., for.) are calling _____ _____

7. they were covering _____ _____

8. were you (pl., for.) adorning? _____ _____

9. if he is drinking _____ _____

10. we were living _____ _____

11. you (s., fam.) were not writing _____ _____

12. I am spending _____ _____

13. if they are studying _____ _____

14. we were spending _____ _____

15. are you (pl., fam.) going up? _____ _____

16. I was opening _____ _____

17. was he running? _____ _____

18. I was not living _____ _____

19. we are not writing _____ _____

Repaso (Future, conditional, progressive)

Write in Spanish:

1. you (pl., for.) will attend _____
   _____

2. I was admiring _____

3. you (s., fam.) will offend _____
   _____

4. I should bother _____

5. you (pl., fam.) are looking for _____
   _____

6. you (s., for.) would not discuss _____
   _____

7. I was insisting _____

8. she is studying _____

9. I will go up _____

10. he would admire _____

11. they were responding _____
    _____

12. he is not bothering _____

13. will they discuss? _____

14. he was working _____

15. you (s., fam.) are not running _____

_____

16. he will listen _____

17. she was entering _____

18. we are spending _____

19. we would cover _____

20. they were cleaning _____

21. I will not open _____

22. you (pl., fam.) would lose _____

_____

23. you (s., for.) are calling _____

_____

24. he will clean _____

25. you (s., fam.) will teach _____

_____

26. you (pl., fam.) are working _____

_____

27. he will throw _____

28. I was writing _____

29. they are drinking _____

30. she would admire _____

31. we were calling _____

32. he was discussing _____

33. I will admire _____

34. you (s., for.) would bother _____

_____

35. they will spend _____

36. you (pl., for.) would write _____

_____

37. they were deciding _____

38. he will respond _____

7 Perfect Tenses

The perfect tenses are compound tenses, consisting in all cases of a form of the verb *haber* plus the past participle.

Past Participle: The past participle of regular verbs is formed by adding *-ado* or *-ido* to the stem.

1	2	3
hablar	**comer**	**partir**
habl *ado* spoken	com *ido* eaten	part *ido* left

The past participle does not change its ending to correspond to person and number in the perfect tenses.

Haber: *to have* is an irregular verb (see pages 112–3) which is used only in idiomatic expressions and as part of the perfect tenses.

Present Perfect: The present perfect is formed with the present tense of *haber* plus the past participle.

yo	*he* hablado I have spoken	*he* comido I have eaten	*he* partido I have left
tú	*has* hablado	*has* comido	*has* partido
Ud.	*ha* hablado	*ha* comido	*ha* partido
él(ella)	*ha* hablado	*ha* comido	*ha* partido
nosotros	*hemos* hablado	*hemos* comido	*hemos* partido
vosotros	*habéis* hablado	*habéis* comido	*habéis* partido
Uds.	*han* hablado	*han* comido	*han* partido
ellos	*han* hablado	*han* comido	*han* partido

Note: The same form of *haber* is used with all three conjugations. Negatives are formed by placing *no* before the *haber* verb.

Pluperfect: The pluperfect (past perfect) is formed with the imperfect of *haber* plus the past participle.

yo *había* hablado   I had spoken
había comido   I had eaten
había partido   I had left

The imperfect of *haber* is formed regularly (see page 8). What are the other forms of the pluperfect of *hablar?*

_____   _____   _____   _____   _____   _____

_____

Future Perfect: The future perfect is formed with the future of *haber* and the past participle.

yo *habré* hablado   I will have spoken
habré comido   I will have eaten
habré partido   I will have left

The future of *haber* is formed by adding the future endings to the stem *habr-*. What are all the forms of the future perfect of *comer?*

_____   _____   _____   _____   _____   _____

_____   _____

What is the English translation of each of the preceding forms? _____

_____

_____

Conditional Perfect: The conditional perfect is formed with the conditional of *haber* and the past
participle.

yo *habría* hablado, comido, partido   I would have spoken, eaten, left

The conditional of *haber* is formed by adding the conditional endings (see page 26) to the future stem *habr-*. What are all the forms of the conditional perfect of *partir?*

_____   _____   _____   _____   _____   _____

_____   _____

What are the English translations? _____

_____

Para practicar

Write the infinitives in (1) the present perfect, (2) pluperfect, (3) future perfect, and (4) conditional perfect, in the subject indicated:

1. yo (aprender)   _____   _____   _____   _____

2. ellos (limpiar)   _____   _____   _____   _____

3. él (vivir)   _____   _____   _____   _____

4. nosotros (comprar)   _____   _____   _____   _____

5. tú (asistir) _____ _____ _____ _____

6. ellos (vender) _____ _____ _____ _____

7. nosotros (tomar) _____ _____ _____ _____

8. él (aprender) _____ _____ _____ _____

9. Ud. (beber) _____ _____ _____ _____

10. ella (contestar) _____ _____ _____ _____

11. vosotros (recibir) _____ _____ _____ _____

12. ellos (preparar) _____ _____ _____ _____

13. nosotros (enseñar) _____ _____ _____ _____

14. tú (temer) _____ _____ _____ _____

15. Ud. (preguntar) _____ _____ _____ _____

16. Uds. (estudiar) _____ _____ _____ _____

17. él (pasar) _____ _____ _____ _____

18. nosotros (subir) _____ _____ _____ _____

19. Uds. (salir) _____ _____ _____ _____

20. tú (guardar) _____ _____ _____ _____

21. yo (esperar) _____ _____ _____ _____

22. vosotros (trabajar) _____ _____ _____ _____

23. ellos (vivir) _____ _____ _____ _____

24. Ud. (partir) _____ _____ _____ _____

25. ella (acabar) _____ _____ _____ _____

Aplicación

Change each simple tense verb to the corresponding perfect tense. Example: *como   he comido;*
hablé or hablaba   había hablado; tomaré   habré tomado, partirías   habrías partido

1. Ud. comprende _____

2. vendías _____

3. escucharon _____

4. subirán _____

5. pregunta _____

6. Ud. discutirá _____

7. aprendían _____

8. Ud. estudió _____

9. escribes _____

10. guardaremos _____

11. admirarían _____

12. echaréis _____

13. temiste _____

14. asisto _____

15. tomábamos _____

16. prepararías _____

17. bebió _____

18. viviremos _____

19. corremos _____

20. viajará _____

21. decidirías _____

22. contestabais _____

23. partisteis _____

24. limpiaré _____

25. molestaríais _____

Mastery Test

Translate into Spanish:

1. I will have learned _____

2. he had cleaned _____

3. we have bought _____

4. they had lived _____

5. he would have run _____

6. I have asked _____

7. you (s., fam.) will have received _____

_____

8. you (s., fam.) had feared _____

_____

9. he has attended _____

10. they would have sold _____

40

11. we will have taken _____

12. you (s., for.) have answered _____

_____

13. I have needed _____

_____

14. you (pl., for.) would have asked _____

_____

15. they have spent _____

16. you (s., fam.) will have discussed _____

_____

17. they have received _____

18. he would have decided _____

_____

19. they will have listened _____

_____

20. we will have entered _____

21. you (s., for.) would have attended _____

_____

22. you (pl., fam.) had understood _____

_____

23. we have lived _____

24. you (pl., for.) will have worked _____

_____

25. he had taken _____

Repaso (Indicative tenses)

Translate into Spanish:

1. you (s., fam.) answer _____

_____

2. they used to live _____

3. I was opening _____

4. you (pl., fam.) are selling _____

_____

5. I will admire _____

6. they did work _____

7. if he asks _____

8. you (pl., for.) will not offend _____

_____

9. we were going up _____

10. if they do not sell _____

11. I should bother _____

12. I was understanding _____

13. we study _____

14. are you (pl., fam.) adorning? _____

_____

15. you (pl., for.) were learning _____

_____

16. we do not live _____

17. you (s., for.) discuss _____

18. he was running _____

19. does she need? _____

20. they bothered _____

21. they did not answer _____

22. she fears _____

23. we insisted _____

24. I did work _____

25. I will throw _____

26. you (pl., fam.) used to prepare _____

_____

27. if he opens _____

28. you (s., for.) were admiring _____

_____

29. they kept _____

30. I will offend _____

31. we were spending _____

32. he would adorn _____

33. we will clean _____

34. we write _____

35. they were covering _____

36. you (pl., for.) were throwing _____

_____

37. they will fear _____

38. I was living _____

39. I used to travel _____

40. you (s., fam.) study _____

41. you (pl., for.) are calling _____

_____

42. you (pl., fam.) would open _____

_____

43. if I drink _____

44. we were insisting _____

45. you (s., fam.) used to write _____

_____

46. will they call? _____

47. I went up _____

48. they would not discuss _____

_____

49. he did understand _____

50. they live _____

8 Present Subjunctive

Present: The present subjunctive of regular verbs is formed in the same way as the present indicative, except that *-ar* verbs use the endings of *-er* verbs, and *-er* and *-ir* verbs use *-ar* endings. All endings are added to the stem.

	1 **hablar**	*2* **comer**	*3* **partir**
yo	habl *e*	com *a*	part *a*
tú	habl *es*	com *as*	part *as*
Ud.	habl *e*	com *a*	part *a*
él(ella)	habl *e*	com *a*	part *a*
nosotros	habl *emos*	com *amos*	part *amos*
vosotros	habl *éis*	com *áis*	part *áis*
Uds.	habl *en*	com *an*	part *an*
ellos	habl *en*	com *an*	part *an*

Note: The present subjunctive may be used as a single clause following ¡*Que...* or ¡*Ojalá que...* to indicate a wish, blessing, or hope:

May you live in peace!	*¡Que viva en paz!*
I hope you live in peace!	*¡Ojalá que viva en paz!*

It is otherwise used in a clause that follows one of certain expressions in the present indicative tense, in which case it is always preceded by *que*. An example we will use here is *Es posible que...*

It's possible that you study	*Es posible que estudies.*
It's possible that you will study.	*Es posible que estudies.*
It's possible that he doesn't understand.	*Es posible que (él) no comprenda.*
It's possible that I (will) attend.	*Es posible que (yo) asista.*

Para practicar

Write the present subjunctive form that corresponds to the subject indicated:

yo

echar	aprender	molestar	emprender	comprender	asistir
_____	_____	_____	_____	_____	_____

vivir

_____

tú

viajar	comprender	llamar	estudiar	beber	abrir
_____	_____	_____	_____	_____	_____

escribir

_____

Ud.

pasar	subir	limpiar	necesitar	vender	escribir
_____	_____	_____	_____	_____	_____

preparar

_____

ella

guardar	abrir	cubrir	contestar	aprender	llamar
_____	_____	_____	_____	_____	_____

tomar

_____

nosotros

preparar	escribir	discutir	preguntar	temer	trabajar
_____	_____	_____	_____	_____	_____

unir

_____

vosotros

trabajar	vivir	insistir	enseñar	leer	pasar
_____	_____	_____	_____	_____	_____

temer

_____

Uds.

responder	admirar	decidir	escuchar	vivir	guardar
_____	_____	_____	_____	_____	_____

viajar

_____

las chicas

correr	adornar	ofender	tomar	recibir	echar
_____	_____	_____	_____	_____	_____

subir

_____

Aplicación

A.   Change from present indicative to present subjunctive.

1. lleva _____

2. vive _____

3. escriben _____

4. trabajáis _____

5. leen _____

6. hablo _____

7. Ud. estudia _____

8. llamamos _____

9. viajas _____

10. abre _____

11. creemos _____

12. manda _____

13. escribes _____

14. tomamos _____

15. comprenden _____

16. como _____

17. vives _____

18. asisto _____

19. Ud. nota _____

20. caminan _____

21. mete _____

22. observáis _____

23. partís _____

24. andas _____

25. insistimos _____

B. Write the present subjunctive form of each verb, as indicated.

¡Ojalá que…!/¡Que…!

1. tú (comprender) _____

2. Ud. (leer) _____

3. yo (recibir) _____

4. Uds. (vender) _____

5. ella (comer) _____

Es posible que …

6. él (cantar) _____

7. yo (estudiar) _____

8. ellos (beber) _____

9. nosotros (tomar) _____

10. vosotros (vivir) _____

11. Ud. (enseñar) _____

12. ellas (correr) _____

Mastery Test

A. Translate into Spanish:

1. It's possible that she doesn't understand _____

2. I hope you (s., fam) study _____

3. May we get _____

4. It's possible that he lives _____

5. I hope they sell _____

46

6. May you (pl., for.) work _____

7. I hope you (pl., fam.) learn _____

8. It's possible that we will teach _____

9. I hope she attends _____

10. It's possible that you will receive _____

B. Translate into Spanish:

1. if he studies _____

2. I hope he studies _____

3. if he sells _____

4. I hope he doesn't sell _____

5. if she learns _____

6. I hope she learns _____

7. if we live _____

8. I hope we live _____

9. if they attend _____

10. I hope they attend _____

9 Imperative

The imperative is used to give commands, and so is always in a form of *you* (unless used to mean *Let's ...*).

For an affirmative command to someone addressed as *tú*, the present indicative tense is used, but the *–s* is dropped:

Speak Spanish!	*¡Habla español!*
Eat with us!	*¡Come con nosotros!*
Write a letter!	*¡Escribe una carta!*

For an affirmative command to those addressed as *vosotros* or *vosotras*, the final *–r* of the infinitive is replaced with *–d*:

Speak Spanish!	*¡Hablad español!*
Eat with us!	*¡Comed con nosotros!*
Write a letter!	*¡Escribid una carta!*

For negative *tú* and *vosotros* commands, the subjunctive is used, as follows:

Tú:	Don't speak English!	*¡No hables inglés!*
	Don't eat with them!	*¡No comas con ellos!*
	Don't write a letter!	*¡No escribas una carta!*

Vosotros/as:	Don't speak English!	*¡No habléis inglés!*
	Don't eat with them!	*¡No comáis con ellos!*
	Don't write a letter!	*¡No escribáis una carta!*

Para practicar

Write the affirmative imperative form of each verb that corresponds to the subject indicated:

tú

viajar	trabajar	estudiar	comer	vender	insistir
_____	_____	_____	_____	_____	_____

vosotros

partir	correr	trabajar	recibir	estudiar	comprar
_____	_____	_____	_____	_____	_____

Write the negative imperative form of each verb that corresponds to the subject indicated:

tú

unir	acabar	comprar	romper	abrir	correr
_____	_____	_____	_____	_____	_____

vosotros

tomar	asistir	preparar	llamar	beber	temer
_____	_____	_____	_____	_____	_____

For both affirmative and negative commands to those addressed as *Ud.*, *Uds.*, and *nosotros*, the subjunctive is used:

Ud.	Speak!	*¡Hable!*	Don't speak!	*¡No hable!*
	Eat!	*¡Coma!*	Don't eat!	*¡No coma!*
	Write!	*¡Escriba!*	Don't write!	*¡No escriba!*
Uds.	Speak!	*¡Hablen!*	Don't speak!	*¡No hablen!*
	Eat!	*¡Coman!*	Don't eat!	*¡No coman!*
	Write!	*¡Escriban!*	Don't write!	*¡No escriban!*
Nosotros	Let's speak!	*¡Hablemos!*	Let's not speak!	*¡No hablemos!*
	Let's eat!	*¡Comamos!*	Let's not eat!	*¡No comamos!*
	Let's write!	*¡Escribamos!*	Let's not write!	*¡No escribamos!*

Para practicar

Write the imperative form of each verb that corresponds to the subject indicated:

Ud.

trabajar	no asistir	contestar	no cantar	abrir	comer
_____	_____	_____	_____	_____	_____

Uds.

no correr	llevar	no meter	no temer	tomar	comprender
_____	_____	_____	_____	_____	_____

nosotros/as

no tomar	estudiar	no contestar	comer	no vender	preparar
_____	_____	_____	_____	_____	_____

An alternative to the affirmative imperative forms for *nosotros/as* is the following:

Vamos a + the infinitive

Let's speak!	*¡Vamos a hablar!*
Let's eat!	*¡Vamos a comer!*
Let's write!	*¡Vamos a escribir!*

There is no equivalent to this for negative commands.

Aplicación

A. Write the command forms as indicated.

1. Llevar (tú) _____

2. Correr (vosotros) _____

3. No comer (Uds.) _____

4. Trabajar (nosotras) _____

5. No abrir (tú) _____

6. No temer (Uds.) _____

7. Comprar (Ud.) _____

8. No preparar (tú) _____

9. Viajar (tú) _____

10. Vender (nosotros) _____

11. No asistir (vosotras) _____

12. Asistir (nosotros) _____

13. Escuchar (Uds.) _____

14. Cocinar (tú) _____

15. No enseñar (Ud.) _____

16. No contestar (tú) _____

17. Echar (vosotros) _____

18. Subir (Uds.) _____

B. Write the following commands in the forms indicated:

1. Don't sell! (tú) _____

2. Eat! (vosotros) _____

3. Don't drink! (Uds.) _____

4. Write! (tú) _____

5. Don't buy! (vosotros) _____

6. Let's buy! (nosotras) _____

7. Let's not study! (nosotros) _____

8. Run! (Uds.) _____

9. Answer! (tú) _____

10. Call! (Ud.) _____

11. Understand! (vosotros) _____

12. Attend! (Uds.) _____

13. Let's ask! (nosotras) _____

14. Teach! (tú) _____

15. Don't open! (tú) _____

16. Travel! (vosotros) _____

17. Reply! (Uds.) _____

18. Go up! (Ud.) _____

10 Imperfect Subjunctive

The imperfect subjunctive is formed by adding either the *-ra* or the *-se* endings, which are listed below, to the stem of the third-person plural preterit indicative.

	1 **hablar** *habla* ron	*2* **comer** *comie* ron	*3* **partir** *partie* ron
	-ra endings		
yo	habla *ra*	comie *ra*	partie *ra*
tú	habla *ras*	comie *ras*	partie *ras*
Ud.	habla *ra*	comie *ra*	partie *ra*
él(ella)	habla *ra*	comie *ra*	partie *ra*
nosotros	hablá *ramos*	comié *ramos*	partié *ramos*
vosotros	habla *rais*	comie *rais*	partie *rais*
Uds.	habla *ran*	comie *ran*	partie *ran*
ellos	habla *ran*	comie *ran*	partie *ran*
	-se endings		
yo	habla *se*	comie *se*	partie *se*
tú	habla *ses*	comie *ses*	partie *ses*
Ud.	habla *se*	comie *se*	partie *se*
él(ella)	habla *se*	comie *se*	partie *se*
nosotros	hablá *semos*	comié *semos*	partié *semos*
vosotros	habla *seis*	comie *seis*	partie *seis*
Uds.	habla *sen*	comie *sen*	partie *sen*
ellos	habla *sen*	comie *sen*	partie *sen*

The first-person plural of both *-ra* and *-se* imperfect subjunctives must have a written accent. There is no difference in meaning between the two forms of the imperfect subjunctive and they may be used interchangeably, although the *-ra* form is the more common.

Note: The imperfect subjunctive is used after *si* and expresses something that is not true or that might not happen; it is followed by a clause in the conditional that indicates what would be or would happen if it were true.

If I studied, I would learn.	*Si yo estudiara, aprendería.*
If he called, she would answer.	*Si él llamara, ella contestaría.*
If she lived here, she would teach Spanish.	*Si ella viviera aquí, enseñaría español.*

Note: The imperfect subjunctive is used after *Ojalá* to express a wish that something were true.

I wish you answered the phone!	*¡Ojalá que contestaras el teléfono!*
I wish you all lived here!	*¡Ojalá que Uds. vivieran aquí!*
I wish he understood!	*¡Ojalá que comprendiera!*

The imperfect subjunctive may also be used in a clause that follows one of certain expressions in the imperfect or preterit, in which case it is always preceded by *que*. Examples we will use here are: *Era posible que…* and *Era imposible que…*

It was possible that you would study.	*Era posible que estudiaras.*
It was impossible that he would understand.	*Era imposible que (él) comprendiera.*
It was possible that I would attend.	*Era posible que (yo) asistiera.*

Para practicar

Write the *-ra* subjunctive form of the following infinitives according to the subject given.

yo

temer	asistir	abrir	acabar	escuchar	necesitar
_____	_____	_____	_____	_____	_____

Ud.

estudiar	abrir	aprender	tener	hablar	enseñar
_____	_____	_____	_____	_____	_____

nosotros

comprender	comer	entrar	partir	vivir	meter
_____	_____	_____	_____	_____	_____

Write these infinitives in the *-se* subjunctive that corresponds to the subject given.

tú

partir	preguntar	vivir	vender	hablar	guardar
_____	_____	_____	_____	_____	_____

ella

enseñar	tomar	comer	aprender	asistir	pasar
_____	_____	_____	_____	_____	_____

Uds.

hablar	contestar	estudiar	tomar	leer	escribir
_____	_____	_____	_____	_____	_____

Aplicación

A. Write the imperfect subjunctive of the verb in the person indicated.

1. él (hablar) _____

2. Elena y yo (vivir) _____

3. nosotros (correr) _____

4. tú (partir) _____

5. yo (pasar) _____

6. vosotros (esperar) _____

7. Uds. (acabar) _____

8. Ud. (caminar) _____

9. él (comprender) _____

10. Juan y Pedro (tomar) _____

11. yo (escribir) _____

12. Ud. (amar) _____

13. tú (beber) _____

14. nosotros (comprar) _____

15. ellos (subir) _____

B. Change from present to imperfect subjunctive.

1. contestemos _____

2. vendas _____

3. pregunte _____

4. aprenda _____

5. escuchen _____

6. Ud. escriba _____

7. aprendan _____

8. Ud. estudie _____

9. vivamos _____

10. tema _____

11. abra _____

12. enseñen _____

13. asista _____

14. tomemos _____

15. Uds. reciban _____

Para practicar

Write the imperfect subjunctive form for each verb, as indicated.

Si...

1. yo (escuchar) _____

2. Uds. (comer) _____

3. ellos (no discutir) _____

4. tú (entrar) _____

5. él (abrir) _____

¡Ojalá que…

6. tú (comprender) _____

7. él (practicar) _____

8. ella (cantar) _____

9. vosotras (escuchar) _____

10. ellos (abrir) _____

Era posible que…

11. Uds. (gastar) _____

12. nosotros (aprender) _____

13. yo (ganar) _____

14. Ud. (no llamar) _____

15. vosotros (escribir) _____

Mastery Test 1

Translate into Spanish:

1. if I taught _____

2. if they lived _____

3. if we went up _____

4. if I didn't understand _____

5. if they took _____

6. if he ran _____

7. if he answered _____

8. if I worked _____

9. if you didn't prepare _____

10. if you (s., for.) studied _____

11. if they kept _____

12. if we didn't spend _____

13. if I travelled _____

14. if you (s., fam.) needed _____

15. if I didn't live _____

16. if you (pl, fam.) opened _____

17. if she wrote _____

18. if you (pl., for.) responded _____

19. if he feared _____

20. if they ate _____

Mastery Test 2

Translate into Spanish:

1. It was possible that they would attend. _____

2. It was impossible that he would sing. _____

3. I wish you (s., fam.) would call! _____

4. If she studied, … _____

5. If they worked, … _____

6. It was impossible that he would clean! _____

7. I wish you spoke. _____

8. If you (pl., fam.) sold … _____

9. It was possible that you (pl., for.) received … _____

10. I wish they answered. _____

11 Perfect Tenses of the Subjunctive

Present Perfect Subjunctive

The *present perfect subjunctive* is formed from the *present* subjunctive of *haber* plus the past participle. The present subjunctive of *haber* is found on page 113.

	1 **hablar**	*2* **comer**	*3* **partir**
yo	*haya* hablado	*haya* comido	*haya* partido
tú	*hayas* hablado	*hayas* comido	*hayas* partido
Ud.	*haya* hablado	*haya* comido	*haya* partido
él(ella)	*haya* hablado	*haya* comido	*haya* partido
nosotros	*hayamos* hablado	*hayamos* comido	*hayamos* partido
vosotros	*hayáis* hablado	*hayáis* comido	*hayáis* partido
Uds.	*hayan* hablado	*hayan* comido	*hayan* partido
ellos	*hayan* hablado	*hayan* comido	*hayan* partido

Note: As with other perfect tenses, the past participle does not change. The person and number of the verb form is indicated only by the *haber* verb.

Second person plural forms must have a written accent.

The negative is formed by placing *no* before the *haber* verb.

Note: The present perfect subjunctive may be used to indicate a past action or event, in a clause that follows one of certain expressions in the present. In such cases, it is always preceded by *que*.

Two examples of these expressions are *Es posible que* and *Es imposible que*

It's possible that you studied.	*Es posible que hayas estudiado.*
It's impossible that he didn't eat.	*Es imposible que (él) no haya comido.*
It's possible that I didn't hear.	*Es posible que (yo) no haya escuchado.*

Pluperfect Subjunctive

The pluperfect subjunctive is formed from the imperfect *(-ra* or *-se)* subjunctive of *haber* plus the past participle. The imperfect subjunctive of *haber* is found on page 113.

	1	*2*	*3*
yo	*hubiera (hubiese)* hablado	*hubiera (hubiese)* comido	*hubiera (hubiese)* partido
tú	*hubieras* hablado	*hubieras* comido	*hubieras* partido
Ud.	*hubiera* hablado	*hubiera* comido	*hubiera* partido
él(ella)	*hubiera* hablado	*hubiera* comido	*hubiera* partido
nosotros	*hubiéramos* hablado	*hubiéramos* comido	*hubiéramos* partido
vosotros	*hubierais* hablado	*hubierais* comido	*hubierais* partido
Uds.	*hubieran* hablado	*hubieran* comido	*hubieran* partido
ellos	*hubieran* hablado	*hubieran* comido	*hubieran* partido

Note: The pluperfect subjunctive is used after *si* to express something that was not true or that did not happen in the past; it is followed by a clause in the conditional perfect that indicates what would have happened if it had been true.

If I had studied, I would have learned.	*Si yo hubiera estudiado, habría aprendido.*
If he had called, she would have answered.	*Si él hubiera llamado, ella habría contestado.*
If she had lived here, she would have taught Spanish.	*Si ella hubiera vivido aquí, habría enseñado español.*

The pluperfect subjunctive is also used in a clause that follows one of certain expressions in the imperfect or preterit. In such cases, it is always preceded by *que*. For practice, three of those expressions are included here: *¡Ojalá que…!, Era posible que* and *Era imposible que:*

I wish we had attended!	*¡Ojalá que hubiéramos asistido!*
It was possible that you studied.	*Era posible que hubieras estudiado.*
It was impossible that he didn't eat.	*Era imposible que (él) no hubiera comido.*
It was possible that I didn't hear.	*Era posible que (yo) no hubiera escuchado.*

Para practicar

Write the *present perfect subjunctive* in the person indicated:

yo (estudiar) _____

María (necesitar) _____

Ud. (viajar) _____

nosotros (pasar) _____

tú (tomar) _____

ellos (vender) _____

tu amigo y tú (asistir) _____

Uds. (llamar) _____

Write in the *pluperfect subjunctive*:

yo (vivir) _____

Uds. (guardar) _____

tú (caminar) _____

ellos (beber) _____

nosotros (echar) _____

vosotros (asistir) _____

Ud. (aprender) _____

Aplicación

Change the following from present subjunctive to present perfect subjunctive.

Example: *coma – haya comido*

1. escuche _____
2. trabajen _____
3. comprendamos _____
4. comprenda _____
5. Ud. corra _____
6. no prepares _____
7. pasemos _____
8. viajéis _____
9. Uds. necesiten _____
10. suba _____
11. no aprendas _____
12. no viva _____

Change the following from imperfect subjunctive to pluperfect subjunctive.

Example: *hablásemos/habláramos – hubiéramos hablado*

13. viviéramos _____
14. guardasen _____
15. viviésemos _____
16. subieras _____
17. no tomase _____
18. respondieran _____
19. estudiarais _____
20. partiera _____
21. temieras _____
22. asistiesen _____
23. no contestara _____
24. discutieses _____

Mastery Test

Translate into Spanish:

1. If I had learned _____

2. It was possible that he had taken _____

3. If she had cleaned _____

4. It is impossible that you (s., fam.) worked _____

5. I wish we had bought _____

6. If we had lived _____

7. I wish they had received _____

8. If you (pl., fam.) had understood _____

9. I wish she had attended _____

10. It is impossible that we took _____

11. If I needed _____

12. If you (s., for.) had asked _____

13. It's possible that they haven't left _____

14. I wish she had won. _____

15. I hope she has entered _____

16. If I had asked _____

17. I wish they listened _____

18. I hope you (pl., fam.) haven't feared _____

19. If she had decided _____

20. I wish you (pl., for.) had answered _____

Repaso del subjuntivo

Write in Spanish:

1. It's possible that you (s., fam.) will write.

_____

2. It's impossible that you (s., fam.) wrote.

_____

3. If you (s., fam.) wrote…

_____

4. I hope you (s., fam.) write.

_____

5. Write! (you, s., fam.)

_____

6. I hope you (s., fam.) have written/wrote.

_____

7. I wish you (s., fam.) would write.

_____

8. I wish you (s., fam.) had written.

_____

9. If he attended …

_____

10. It was impossible that she understood.

_____

11. It is possible that they argued.

_____

12. I hope you eat.

_____

13. I hope you (pl., for.) answered.

_____

14. If we travelled …

_____

15. I hope you (pl., fam.) have read

_____

16. If they ran …

_____

17. It is possible that she will speak

_____

18. May you (pl., for.) insist

_____

19. May we live in peace!

_____

20. It was impossible that she would answer.

_____

12 Reflexive Verbs

Reflexive verbs are verbs in which the object is the same person as the subject, that is, the subject does the action to itself. Therefore, in Spanish reflexive verbs, the object pronoun must change each time the person of the subject changes. The reflexive verb has the same forms as a nonreflexive verb, but the object pronoun is always included, in the same person as the ending of the verb indicates.

Present of Reflexive Verbs: levantar (se)   to get (oneself) up, to arise

yo	*me* levanto	I get (myself) up	nosotros	*nos* levantamos	we get (ourselves) up
tú	*te* levantas	you get (yourself) up	vosotros	*os* levantáis	you get (yourselves) up
Ud.	*se* levanta	you get (yourself) up	Uds.	*se* levantan	you get (yourselves) up
él	*se* levanta	he gets (himself) up	ellos	*se* levantan	they get (themselves) up
ella	*se* levanta	she gets (herself) up	ellas	*se* levantan	they get (themselves) up

Reflexive pronouns are the same for verbs of all three conjugations. The infinitive indicates that the verb is reflexive by having *-se* attached to it (*levantarse*). The *se* is removed with the infinitive ending when the personal endings are attached. The reflexive is also the same form for all tenses of the verb.

Imperfect: yo me levantaba   I was getting up. Write the other forms of the imperfect of *levantarse,* taking care to use the correct reflexive pronoun with each form (Imperfect, p. 8):

_____   _____   _____   _____

_____   _____   _____   _____

Preterit: yo me levanté   I got up. Write the other forms of the preterit of *levantarse* (p. 13):

_____   _____   _____   _____

_____   _____   _____   _____

Future: yo me levantaré   I shall get up. Write the other forms of the future of *levantarse* (p. 20):

_____   _____   _____   _____

_____   _____   _____   _____

Conditional: yo me levantaría   I would get up. Write the other forms of the conditional of *levantarse* (p. 26):

_____   _____   _____   _____

_____   _____   _____   _____

Progressive Tenses: *yo me estoy levantando* or *yo estoy levantándome*   I am getting up.
   Note that the pronoun may either precede or follow in the progressive. Write the *yo* form of the *past* progressive of *levantarse* in Spanish and translate into English:

yo _____   _____

Perfect Tenses: *Present*: *yo me he levantado*   I have gotten up. The pronoun precedes the *haber* verb in all perfect tenses. Write the (1) pluperfect, (2) future perfect, and (3) conditional perfect of *levantarse,* and translate each into English:

yo me he levantado: Translate:

(1) yo _____   (1) _____

(2) _____   (2) _____

(3) _____   (3) _____

Subjunctive: Present: yo me levante   Es posible que yo me levante.   It's possible that I will get up. Write the other forms of present subjunctive:

Es posible que ...

_____   _____   _____   _____

_____   _____

Imperfect: *yo me levantara* (*me levantase*)   *Era imposible que yo me levantara.* It was impossible for me to get up. (lit, that I would get up) Write the other forms of the imperfect subjunctive, first the *-ra* and then the *-se* forms:

Era imposible que …

tú _____   tú (-se) _____

Ud. _____   Ud. _____

él _____   él _____

_____   _____

_____   _____

_____   _____

Present Perfect: yo me haya levantado   Es posible que yo me haya levantado.   It's possible that I got up.
Write the singular forms of the present perfect subjunctive and translate into English:

Es posible que …

yo _____   Trans. _____

tú _____   _____

Ud. _____   _____

él _____   _____

Pluperfect: yo me hubiera levantado   Si yo me hubiera levantado   If I had gotten up. Write the plural forms
of the imperfect subjunctive (*-se* form) and translate into English:

Era imposible que …

nosotros _____   Trans. _____

vosotros _____   _____

Uds. _____   _____

ellos _____   _____

Aplicación

Two other verbs which are treated in a manner similar to *levantarse* are *lavarse*   to wash up (to wash
oneself), and *peinarse*   to comb one's hair (to comb oneself).

A.   Add reflexive pronouns so that the verbs
express the idea of a subject acting on itself.

1. lavéis _____

2. peinaban _____

3. levantó _____

4. peinemos _____

5. levantábamos _____

6. lavan _____

7. levantamos _____

8. hayan peinado _____

B.   Change each simple tense to a corresponding
compound tense, keeping the person of the
original verb.

1. se levanten _____

2. nos levantamos _____

3. te peinas _____

4. os levantáis _____

5. nos peinaremos _____

6. me peiné _____

7. se levantaba _____

8. nos levantaríamos _____

9. lavabas _____

10. peiné _____

11. lavantáis _____

12. hubieras levantado _____

13. peina _____

14. lavaré _____

15. peinarías _____

9. se peinaron _____

10. se lave _____

11. os peinéis _____

12. nos lavemos _____

13. me levante _____

14. se levantarán _____

15. me lavaré _____

Mastery Test

Write in Spanish, using reflexive verbs:

1. I hope he has washed up _____

2. they were washing _____

3. they comb their hair _____

4. It was possible that he would wash up _____

5. I had gotten up _____

6. they got up _____

7. they will have washed _____

8. I am combing my hair _____

9. they would have gotten up _____

10. I used to get up _____

11. I wash _____

12. It's possible that she will get up _____

13. We will wash up _____

14. He has washed up _____

15. It was impossible for us to comb our hair _____

16. they washed up _____

17. I would wash up _____

18. they get up _____

19. you (s., fam.) washed up _____

20. It was impossible for them to wash up _____

Repaso de verbos regulares

A.   Change each verb to represent more than one person in the same tense. Example: *hablo - hablamos*

1. acabo _____

2. comprendiste _____

3. él temía _____

4. necesitaré _____

5. partirías _____

6. estoy enseñando _____

7. partes _____

8. Ud. hable _____

9. ha enseñado _____

10. hayas hablado _____

11. estaba lavándose _____

12. habías vendido _____

13. él hubiese asistido _____

14. bebieras _____

15. habrá preguntado _____

16. habrías tomado _____

17. escucha _____

18. he estudiado _____

19. habrás temido _____

20. aprenderá _____

21. comprendas _____

22. está viviendo _____

23. Ud. había acabado _____

24. contesté _____

25. Ud. vendiese _____

26. yo habría partido _____

27. abrías _____

28. Ud. entraría _____

29. estabas comiendo _____

30. Ud. haya tomado _____

B. Translate into English:

1. parto _____

2. Uds. escribieron _____

3. asistiréis _____

4. ellos vivían _____

5. tomaríamos _____

6. enseñasteis _____

7. él está estudiando _____

8. temeremos _____

9. Ud. estaba abriendo _____

_____

10. ella vendería _____

11. has asistido _____

12. Ud. ha comido _____

13. ellos habían comprendido _____

_____

14. estás escuchando _____

15. habremos tenido _____

16. yo había estudiado _____

17. estaba levantándome _____

_____

18. habrás hablado _____

19. si bebiéramos _____

20. Ud. habría contestado _____

_____

21. comas _____

22. él escriba _____

23. es imposible que él se haya lavado _____

24. si aprendiésemos _____

25. si hubieras estudiado _____

26. Ojalá que hayáis hablado _____

27. si Uds. hubieran comido _____

_____

28. ellos temen _____

29. Uds. habrían llevado _____

30. Uds. llevaban _____

C. Write in Spanish:

1. they fear _____

2. if she had left _____

3. you (s., fam.) used to eat _____

4. it is possible that we spoke _____

5. did you (pl., fam.) speak? _____

6. I used to leave _____

7. we will learn _____

8. it was possible that you (s., fam.) would take _____

9. he would not write _____

10. they understood _____

11. you (s., fam.) are answering _____

12. they would have left _____

13. you (pl., fam.) were speaking _____

14. I have studied _____

15. do not finish! (pl., fam.) _____

16. they had left _____

17. I will have taught _____

18. you (s., for.) will have lived _____

19. we are living _____

20. you (pl., for.) would have taught _____

21. let us fear _____

22. you (s., fam.) do not read _____

23. it was possible that he would sell _____

24. it is possible that you (pl., fam.) haven't eaten _____

25. he was selling _____

26. it was possible that you (pl., fam.) didn't listen _____

27. I sell _____

28. will you (s., fam.) read? _____

29. they used to carry _____

30. you (s., fam.) wrote _____

31. you (pl., fam.) will attend _____

32. we would take _____

33. she is not studying _____

34. you (pl., fam.) were opening _____

35. you (s., for.) have not attended _____

36. I had understood _____

37. you (s., fam.) would carry _____

38. they will have studied _____

39. you (pl., for.) would not have needed _____

40. drink! (pl., for.) _____

41. it was possible that we wouldn't attend _____

42. you (s., fam.) have lived _____

43. it's possible that he hasn't finished _____

44. it was possible that you learned _____

45. do you (pl., fam.) open? _____

46. I used to fear _____

47. you (s., fam.) had taken _____

48. they asked _____

49. you (s., for.) will enter _____

50. would you (s., fam.) read? _____

13 Stem-Changing Verbs—Class I

Stem-changing verbs change the last vowel of the stem under certain conditions.

In stem-changing verbs of Class I (*-ar* or *-er* verbs), the *e* or *o* of the stem changes to *ie* or *ue,* respectively, in all the forms, except *nosotros* and *vosotros,* of both the present indicative and the present subjunctive.

Present Indicative:

	1			*2*	
	pensar to think			**entender** to understand	
yo	*piens* o	I think, am thinking		*entiend* o	I understand, etc.
tú	*piens* as			*entiend* es	
Ud.	*piens* a			*entiend* e	
él(ella)	*piens* a			*entiend* e	
nosotros	pens amos			entend emos	
vosotros	pens áis			entend éis	
Uds.	*piens* an			*entiend* en	
ellos	*piens* an			*entiend* en	

Present Subjunctive:

	1			*2*	
	contar to tell			**volver** to return	
yo	*cuent* e	I may tell		*vuelv* a	I may return
tú	*cuent* es			*vuelv* as	
Ud.	*cuent* e			*vuelv a*	
él(ella)	*cuent* e			*vuelv* a	
nosotros	cont emos			volv amos	
vosotros	cont éis			volv áis	
Uds.	*cuent* en			*vuelv* an	
ellos	*cuent* en			*vuelv* an	

What would the present subjunctive of (1) *pensar* (2) *entender* be?

(1) _____ _____ _____ _____ _____ _____

_____ _____

(2) _____ _____ _____ _____ _____ _____

_____ _____

What would the present indicative of (1) *contar* and (2) *volver* be?

(1) _____ _____ _____ _____ _____ _____

_____ _____

(2) _____ _____ _____ _____ _____ _____

_____ _____

Other Verbs of Class I:

calentar   to warm
cerrar   to close
mostrar   to show
morder   to bite
perder   to lose
mover   to move
revolver   to stir, turnover

devolver   to give back, return
encender   to light
acertar   to succeed, guess right
acordar   to agree
acostar(se)   to put (go) to bed
aprobar   to approve
sentar(se)   to seat (sit)

confesar   to confess
costar   to cost
*nevar**   to snow
*llover**   to rain
encontrar   to find, meet

* This verb is used only in the third-person singular.

Para practicar

A.   Write the verb in the *present indicative* in the subject indicated:

yo

cerrar	encontrar	mostrar	perder	revolver	encender
_____	_____	_____	_____	_____	_____

Uds.

confesar	acostarse	mover	devolver	acertar	acordar
_____	_____	_____	_____	_____	_____

nosotros

sentarse	contar	mostrar	perder	devolver	entender
_____	_____	_____	_____	_____	_____

B. Write the verbs in the *present subjunctive* in the subject indicated:

tú

contar	pensar	morder	aprobar	devolver	entender
_____	_____	_____	_____	_____	_____

ellas

cerrar	encontrar	mostrar	perder	mover	encender
_____	_____	_____	_____	_____	_____

vosotros

entender	revolver	mostrar	mover	confesar	acordar
_____	_____	_____	_____	_____	_____

72

Mastery Test

A. Translate into English:

1. se acuestan _____

2. me acuerdo _____

3. ella vuelve _____

4. Ud. caliente _____

5. mostremos _____

6. perdéis _____

7. que Uds. revuelvan _____

8. enciendas _____

9. él aprobó _____

10. me sentaba _____

11. costó _____

12. nevará _____

13. confieso _____

14. ellos devuelven _____

15. cierre Ud. _____

B. Translate into Spanish:

1. you (pl., fam.) lost _____

2. I hope that they understand _____
_____

3. it's possible that we will meet _____

4. do you (s., fam.) close? _____
_____

5. you (s., fam.) do not understand _____
_____

6. they moved _____

7. I was moving _____

8. they may show _____

9. you (s., fam.) move _____

10. we warmed _____

11. I am lighting _____

12. they do not lose _____

13. I may bite _____

14. I hope that you (s., fam.) will stir _____
_____

15. it costs _____

14 Stem-Changing Verbs—Class II

In stem-changing verbs of Class II (*-ir* verbs), the *e* or *o* of the stem changes to *ie* or *ue* respectively, in all the forms of the present indicative tense, except the *nosotros* and *vosotros* forms, and to *i* or *u* in the third-person singular and plural of the preterit. In the present subjunctive, the *ie* and *ue* change to *i* and *u*, respectively, in the *nosotros* and *vosotros* forms.

Present:	**sentir** to feel		**dormir** to sleep	
yo	*sient* o	I feel, am feeling	*duerm* o	I sleep, am sleeping
tú	*sient* es		*duerm* es	
Ud.	*sient* e		*duerm* e	
él(ella)	*sient* e		*duerm* e	
nosotros	sent imos		dorm imos	
vosotros	sent ís		dorm ís	
Uds.	*sient* en		*duerm* en	
ellos	*sient* en		*duerm* en	

Present Participle: *sint* iendo feeling   *durm* iendo sleeping

Preterit:

yo	sent í	I felt, did feel	dorm í	I slept, did sleep
tú	sent iste		dorm iste	
Ud.	*sint* ió		*durm* ió	
él(ella)	*sint* ió		*durm* ió	
nosotros	sent imos		dorm imos	
vosotros	sent isteis		dorm isteis	
Uds.	*sint* ieron		*durm* ieron	
ellos	*sint* ieron		*durm* ieron	

No other tenses of the indicative are affected.

Present Subjunctive:

yo	*sient* a	I may feel		*duerm* a	I may sleep
tú	*sient* as			*duerm* as	
Ud.	*sient* a			*duerm* a	
él(ella)	*sient* a			*duerm* a	
nosotros	*sint* amos			*durm* amos	
vosotros	*sint* áis			*durm* áis	
Uds.	*sient* an			*duerm* an	
ellos	*sient* an			*duerm* an	

Imperfect Subjunctive: Since the imperfect subjunctive is formed from the stem of the third-person plural preterit, all forms reflect the same stem-change.

yo	*sint* iera	*sint* iese	I might	*durm* iera	*durm* iese	I might
tú	*sint* ieras	*sint* ieses	feel	*durm* ieras	*durm* ieses	sleep
Ud.	*sint* iera	*sint* iese		*durm* iera	*durm* iese	
él(ella)	*sint* iera	*sint* iese		*durm* iera	*durm* iese	
nosotros	*sint* iéramos	*sint* iésemos		*durm* iéramos	*durm* iésemos	
vosotros	*sint* ierais	*sint* ieseis		*durm* ierais	*durm* ieseis	
Uds.	*sint* ieran	*sint* iesen		*durm* ieran	*durm* iesen	
ellos	*sint* ieran	*sint* iesen		*durm* ieran	*durm* iesen	

Others:

advertir	to notice	*mentir*	to lie
consentir	to spoil, consent	*morir*	to die
divertir(se)	to amuse (oneself), have fun	*herir*	to wound

Para practicar

Change the verbs to the tense and person indicated:

Present indicative   **tú**

advertir	mentir	morir	herir	consentir
_____	_____	_____	_____	_____

Present Subjunctive   **Ud.**

divertirse	sentir	dormir	mentir	morir
_____	_____	_____	_____	_____

Preterit **ellos**

herir	advertir	divertirse	dormir	consentir
_____	_____	_____	_____	_____

Imperfect Subjunctive **nosotros**

morir	sentir	mentir	dormir	advertir
_____	_____	_____	_____	_____

Present Participle

morir	herir	consentir	advertir	divertirse
_____	_____	_____	_____	_____

Mastery Test

A. Translate into English:

1. Ud. mentía _____

2. dormimos _____

3. ella murió _____

4. si ellos mintieran _____

5. él había sentido _____

6. ellos se divierten _____

7. él hirió _____

8. es imposible que él consienta _____

9. no advierto _____

10. Uds. mintieron _____

11. sentí _____

12. ojalá que duermas _____

13. sintáis _____

14. ellos duerman _____

15. nos divirtamos _____

B. Translate into Spanish:

1. they do not wound _____

2. you (s., fam.) have slept _____

   _____

3. it's possible that we will spoil _____

   _____

4. if I died _____

5. I hope he sleeps _____

6. you (s., fam.) amused yourself _____

   _____

7. we will lie _____

8. they were dying _____

9. he was feeling _____

10. if he slept, … _____

11. I would spoil _____

12. you (s., for.) noticed _____

13. I sleep _____

14. if they felt… _____

15. I hope you (pl., for.) amuse yourselves _____

   _____

15 Stem-Changing Verbs—Class III

In stem-changing verbs of Class III (*-ir* verbs), the *e* of the stem changes to *i* in all the forms of the present indicative tense, except the *nosotros* and *vosotros* forms, and in the third-person singular and plural of the preterit.

Pedir   to ask for

Present Indicative: *pido, pides, pide,* pedimos, pedís, *piden*   I ask for, etc.

Imperfect: pedía, etc.   I was looking for, etc.

Preterit: pedí, pediste, *pidió,* pedimos, pedisteis, *pidieron*   I asked for, etc.

Future: pediré, etc.   I will ask for, etc.

Conditional: pediría, etc.   I would ask for, etc.

Present Participle: *pidiendo*   asking for

Past Participle: pedido

Present Subjunctive: *pida, pidas, pida, pidamos, pidáis, pidan*   that I ask for/will ask for, etc.

Imperfect Subjunctive: *pidiera* (*pidiese*), etc.   that I asked for/would ask for, etc.

Present Perfect Subjunctive: haya pedido, etc.   that I (have) asked for, etc.

Pluperfect Subjunctive: hubiera (hubiese) pedido, etc.   that I had asked for/would have asked for, etc.;
if I had asked for, etc.

All Spanish forms not in italics are regular.

Others:

impedir to prevent	*gemir* to groan
repetir to repeat	*medir* to measure
servir to serve	*competir* to compete
vestirse to get dressed, dress	

Para practicar

Change the verbs to the tense and person indicated:

Present indicative   **Ud.**

impedir	competir	servir	medir
_____	_____	_____	_____

Present subjunctive   **vosotros**

gemir	pedir	impedir	competir
_____	_____	_____	_____

Preterit **ellos**

vestirse	servir	medir	impedir
_____	_____	_____	_____

Mastery Test

Translate into English:

1. que ellos gimieran _____
2. que me vista _____
3. él pediría _____
4. medíamos _____
5. midáis _____
6. impedimos _____
7. Ud. gimió _____
8. competiré _____

9. sirviéramos _____
10. él gime _____
11. mediste _____
12. sirvieron _____
13. compito _____
14. se visten _____
15. que impidas _____

Repaso (Stem-changing verbs)

A. Write the *third-person singular present indicative* of the following verbs:

ella

gemir	competir	cerrar	sentir	impedir	mostrar
_____	_____	_____	_____	_____	_____

encontrar	divertirse	sentarse	revolver
_____	_____	_____	_____

B. Write the *first-person plural present subjunctive* of the following verbs:

nosotros

aprobar	medir	dormir	confesar	mentir	advertir
_____	_____	_____	_____	_____	_____

pedir	vestirse	repetir	consentir
_____	_____	_____	_____

C. Write in Spanish:

1. they understand _____

2. that we spoil/will spoil _____

3. that I dress/will dress _____

4. he is not amusing himself _____

_____

5. that we close/will close _____

6. you (s., fam.) asked for _____

_____

7. she did not notice _____

8. he meets _____

9. that you (s., fam.) groaned/would groan _____

_____

10. that I die/will die _____

11. that you (s., fam.) move/will move _____

_____

12. that we served/would serve _____

13. they notice _____

14. I close _____

15. he competes _____

16. that you (s., fam.) show/will show _____

_____

17. that I amused/would amuse myself _____

_____

18. they served _____

19. you (pl., fam.) do not lose _____

_____

20. that she sleeps/will sleep _____

21. he prevents _____

22. that I give back/will give back _____

23. they felt _____

24. that you (pl., for.) prevent/will prevent _____

_____

25. does he understand? _____

26. they are not dying _____

27. she did not compete _____

28. that it snows/will snow _____

29. you (s., fam.) are lying _____

_____

30. that they asked for/would ask for _____

16 Orthographic Changes

Orthographic-changing verbs change the spelling of certain consonants when it is necessary to maintain a uniform pronunciation of their stems.

Verbs ending in -car change *c* to *qu* before the letter *e.*

Buscar to look for

Present Indicative: busco, etc. I look for, etc. (p. 1)

Imperfect: buscaba, etc. I was looking for, etc. (p. 8)

Preterit: *busqué,* buscaste, buscó, etc. I looked for, etc. (p. 13)

Future: buscaré, etc. I will look for, etc. (p. 20)

Conditional: buscaría, etc. I would look for, etc. (p. 26)

Present Participle: buscando looking for

Past Participle: buscado looked for

Present Subjunctive: *busque, busques, busque, busquemos, busquéis, busquen* that I look for/will look for, etc.

Imperfect Subjunctive: buscara (buscase), etc. that I looked/would look for, etc.; if I looked for, etc. (p. 46)

Present Perfect Subjunctive: haya buscado, etc. that I (have) looked for, etc. (p. 49)

Pluperfect Subjunctive: hubiera (hubiese) buscado, etc. that I had looked for/would have looked for, etc.; if I had looked for, etc. (p. 49)

Verb forms not in italics are not affected.

Others:

colocar to place	*sacar* to take out
explicar to explain	*secar* to dry
indicar to indicate	*convocar* to call together
marcar to mark	*replicar* to reply
mascar (masticar) to chew	*pecar* to sin
rascar to scratch	

Verbs ending in -*gar* change *g* to *gu* before the letter *e.* The *u* is not pronounced.

Pagar to pay

Present Indicative: pago, pagas, etc. I pay, etc.

Imperfect: pagaba, etc. I was paying, etc.

Preterit: *pagué,* pagaste, pagó, etc. I paid, etc.

Future: pagaré, etc. I will pay, etc.

Conditional: pagaría, etc. I would pay, etc.

Present Participle: pagando paying

Past Participle: pagado paid

Present Subjunctive: *pague, pagues, pague, paguemos, paguéis, paguen* that I pay (for)/will pay (for), etc.

Imperfect Subjunctive: pagara (pagase) that I paid (for)/would pay (for), etc.; if I paid (for), etc.

Present Perfect Subjunctive: haya pagado, etc.   that I (have) paid (for), etc.

Pluperfect Subjunctive: hubiera (hubiese) pagado, etc.   that I had paid (for)/would have paid (for), etc.; if I had paid for, etc.

Others:

apagar to turn off, extinguish	*llegar* to arrive
arriesgar to risk	*obligar* to oblige
cargar to load	*vagar* to wander
castigar to punish	*colgar** to hang up
ahogar to drown	*rogar** to beg, ask
entregar to hand over	*negar** to deny
fatigar to tire	*cegar** to blind

* see page 93

Verbs ending in *-zar* change *z* to *c* before the letter *e*.

Rezar   to pray

Present Indicative: rezo, rezas, etc.   I pray, etc.

Imperfect: rezaba, etc.   I was praying, etc.

Preterit: recé, rezaste, rezó, etc.   I prayed, etc.

Future: rezaré, etc.   I will pray, etc.

Conditional: rezaría, etc.   I would pray, etc.

Present Participle: rezando   praying

Past Participle: rezado   prayed

Present Subjunctive: *rece, reces, rece, recemos, recéis, recen,*   that I pray/will pray, etc.

Imperfect Subjunctive: rezara (rezase), etc.   that I prayed/would pray, etc.; if I prayed, etc.

Present Perfect Subjunctive: haya rezado, etc.   that I (have) prayed, etc.

Pluperfect Subjunctive: hubiera (hubiese) rezado, etc.   that I had prayed/would have prayed, etc.; if I had prayed, etc.

Others:

abrazar to embrace	*rechazar* to reject
alcanzar to reach, achieve	*sollozar* to sob
amenazar to threaten	*empezar** to begin
analizar to analyze	*almorzar** to eat lunch
cruzar to cross	*tropezar** to stumble
lanzar to throw	

* see page 93

Verbs ending in *-guar* change *gu* to *gü* before *e*. The *u* requires a diaeresis (¨) before *e* to preserve the *u* sound.

Averiguar   to find out, verify

Present Indicative: averiguo, etc.   I find out, etc.

Imperfect: averiguaba, etc.   I was finding out, etc.

Preterit: averigüé, averiguaste, averiguó, etc.   I found out, etc.

Future: averiguaré, etc.   I will find out, etc.

Conditional: averiguaría, etc.   I would find out, etc.

Present Participle: averiguando   finding out

Past Participle: averiguado   found out

Present Subjunctive: *averigüe, averigües, averigüe, averigüemos, averigüéis, averigüen*   that I find out/will find out, etc.

Imperfect Subjunctive: averiguara (averiguase), etc.   that I found out/would find out, etc.; if I found out, etc.

Present Perfect Subjunctive: haya averiguado, etc.   that I (have) found out, etc.

Pluperfect Subjunctive: hubiera (hubiese) averiguado, etc.   that I had found out/would have found out, etc.; if I had found out, etc.

Others:

apaciguar   to pacify

menguar   to decrease

santiguar   to bless

Para practicar

Write in the *present subjunctive* in the person indicated:

tú:

secar	colocar	obligar	entregar	amenazar	analizar
_____	_____	_____	_____	_____	_____

averiguar	menguar
_____	_____

ellos

alcanzar	abrazar	llegar	castigar	arriesgar	rascar
_____	_____	_____	_____	_____	_____

replicar	explicar
_____	_____

Write in the *first-person singular preterit indicative*:

yo

explicar	sacar	indicar	negar	llegar	castigar
_____	_____	_____	_____	_____	_____

rogar	replicar	empezar	cruzar	rechazar	almorzar
_____	_____	_____	_____	_____	_____

marcar	apaciguar	santiguar
_____	_____	_____

Mastery Test

A. Translate into English:

1. que él explique _____

2. si Ud. marcara _____

3. que yo apague _____

4. abracé _____

5. entregué _____

6. que tropecemos _____

7. que ellos sequen _____

8. que castigues _____

9. que Ud. rechace _____

10. que averigües _____

11. que tú repliques _____

12. que carguemos _____

13. que amenaces _____

14. que ella entregue _____

15. saqué _____

16. que santigüemos _____

17. que él llegue _____

18. que Uds. analicen _____

B. Translate into Spanish:

1. I hope we pacify _____

2. 1 paid _____

3. it's possible that they will take out _____

_____

4. I did not find out _____

5. it's possible that he will punish _____

_____

6. it's possible that he won't place _____

_____

7. I risked _____

8. I hope we don't tire (get tired) _____

_____

9. it's possible that she won't reply _____

_____

10. it's possible that you (s., fam.) will cross _____

_____

11. I hope you (pl., fam.) don't beg _____

_____

A. Translate into English: (*continued*)

19. que apacigüen _____

20. que él alcance _____

B. Translate into Spanish: (*continued*)

12. I indicated _____

13. he prays _____

14. I hope you (s., fam.) throw _____

_____

15. I hope they arrive _____

16. I did not explain _____

17. it's impossible that we analyze (for us to analyze) ____

_____

18. I hope that you (pl., for.) reply _____

_____

19. I threw _____

20. I sobbed _____

Some verbs ending in *-cer* and *-cir* preceded by a consonant change *c* to *z* before *o* or *a*.

Vencer   to conquer

Present Indicative: *venzo,* vences, etc.   I conquer, etc.

Imperfect: vencía, etc.   I was conquering, etc.

Preterit: vencí, etc.   I conquered, etc.

Future: venceré, etc.   I will conquer, etc.

Conditional: vencería, etc.   I would conquer, etc.

Present Participle: venciendo   conquering

Past Participle: vencido   conquered

Present Subjunctive: *venza, venzas, venza, venzamos, venzáis, venzan*   that I conquer/will conquer, etc.

Imperfect Subjunctive: venciera, (venciese), etc.   that I conquered/would conquer, etc.; if I conquered, etc.

Present Perfect Subjunctive: haya vencido, etc.   that I (have) conquered, etc.

Pluperfect Subjunctive: hubiera (hubiese) vencido, etc.   that I had conquered/would have conquered, etc.; if I had conquered, etc.

Others:
convencer   to convince
ejercer   to exercise
esparcir   to scatter

Verbs ending in *-ger* or *-gir* change *g* to *j* before an *o* or *a*.

Escoger   to choose

Present Indicative: *escojo,* escoges, etc.   I choose, etc.

Imperfect: escogía, etc.   I was choosing, etc.

Preterit: escogí, etc.   I chose, etc.

Future: escogeré, etc.   I will choose, etc.

Conditional: escogería, etc.   I would choose, etc.

Present Participle: escogiendo   choosing

Past Participle: escogido   chosen

Present Subjunctive: *escoja, escojas, escoja, escojamos, escojáis, escojan*   that I choose/will choose, etc.

Imperfect Subjunctive: escogiera (escogiese), etc.   that I chose/would choose, etc.; if I chose, etc.

Present Perfect Subjunctive: haya escogido, etc.   that I chose/have chosen, etc.

Pluperfect Subjunctive: hubiera (hubiese) escogido, etc.   that I had chosen/would have chosen, etc.; if I had chosen, etc.

Others:
dirigir to direct	*acoger* to welcome
coger to catch, seize, take	*encoger* to shrink
fingir to pretend	*corregir* to correct*
exigir to demand	*elegir* to elect, choose*
infligir to inflict	

* see page 94

Verbs ending in *-guir* drop the *u* before *o* or *a*.

Distinguir   to distinguish

Present Indicative: *distingo,* distingues, etc.   I distinguish, etc.

Imperfect: distinguía, etc.   I was distinguishing, etc.

Preterit: distinguí, etc.   I distinguished, etc.

Future: distinguiré, etc.   I will distinguish, etc.

Conditional: distinguiría, etc.   I would distinguish, etc.

Present Participle: distinguiendo   distinguishing

Past Participle: distinguido   distinguished

Present Subjunctive: *distinga, distingas, distinga, distingamos, distingáis, distingan*   that I distinguish/will distinguish, etc.

Imperfect Subjunctive: distinguiera (distinguiese) etc.   that I distinguished/would distinguish, etc.; if I distinguished, etc.

Present Perfect Subjunctive: haya distinguido, etc.   that I (have) distinguished, etc.

Pluperfect Subjunctive: hubiera (hubiese) distinguido, etc.   that I had distinguished/would have distinguished, etc.; if I had distinguished, etc.

Others:

extinguir to extinguish	*perseguir* to persecute, pursue*
seguir to follow*	*proseguir* to prosecute, pursue*
conseguir to get, obtain*	

* see page 94

Verbs ending in *-quir* change *qu* to *c* before *o* or *a*.

Delinquir   to break the law

Present Indicative: *delinco,* delinques, etc.   I break the law, etc.

Imperfect: delinquía, etc.   I was breaking the law, etc.

Preterit: delinquí, etc.   I broke the law, etc.

Future: delinquiré, etc.   I will break the law, etc.

Conditional: delinquiría, etc.   I would break the law, etc.

Present Participle: delinquiendo   breaking the law

Past Participle: delinquido   broken the law

Present Subjunctive: *delinca, delincas, delinca, delincamos, delincáis, delincan*   that I break the law/will break the law, etc.

Imperfect Subjunctive: delinquiera (delinquiese), etc.   that I broke the law/would break the law, etc.; if I broke the law, etc.

Present Perfect Subjunctive: haya delinquido, etc.   that I broke/have broken the law, etc.

Pluperfect Subjunctive: hubiera (hubiese) delinquido, etc.   that I had broken/would have broken the law, etc.; if I had broken the law, etc.

Para practicar

Write the verbs in the tense and person indicated:

Present indicative   **yo**

encoger	dirigir	coger	exigir	ejercer	convencer
_____	_____	_____	_____	_____	_____

esparcir	extinguir	delinquir	acoger
_____	_____	_____	_____

Present subjunctive   **nosotros**

extinguir	delinquir	distinguir	escoger	infligir	fingir
_____	_____	_____	_____	_____	_____

coger	esparcir	ejercer	dirigir
_____	_____	_____	_____

Aplicación

Translate into English:

1. ejerzo _____

2. Ud. convenció _____

3. esparciré _____

4. acogías _____

5. que ellos distingan _____

6. que finjamos _____

7. Uds. han convencido _____

8. dirigiré _____

9. él seguiría _____

10. que extingas _____

11. ejercías _____

12. exijo _____

13. seguí _____

14. extinguiste _____

15. que ellos convenzan _____

16. fingí _____

17. él delinquió _____

18. que ellos recojan _____

19. extingo _____

20. delincáis _____

Mastery Test

Translate into Spanish:

1. if you (s., fam.) conquered _____

2. it's possible that I will inflict _____

3. I distinguish _____

4. we exercised _____

5. I do not demand _____

6. I hope that you (s., fam.) don't distinguish _____

7. he will not convince _____

8. will you (pl., for.) choose? _____

9. let us not extinguish _____

10. I scattered _____

11. we directed _____

12. he distinguished _____

13. I break the law _____

14. you (s., fam.) exercise _____

15. I hope that he will welcome _____

16. it's possible that they will extinguish _____

17. it's possible that they won't convince _____

18. I pretend _____

19. you (pl., fam.) will distinguish _____

20. I hope that you don't break the law _____.

Verbs ending in -eer change the i to y in the third-person singular and plural of the preterit, all persons of the imperfect subjunctive and the present participle.

Creer   to believe

Present Indicative: creo, etc.   I believe, etc.

Imperfect: creía, etc.   I was believing, etc.

Preterit: creí, creíste, *creyó,* creímos, creísteis, *creyeron*   I believed, etc.

Future: creeré, etc.   I will believe, etc.

Conditional: creería, etc.   I would believe, etc.

Present Participle: *creyendo*   believing

Past Participle: creído   believed

Present Subjunctive: crea, etc.   that I believe/will believe, etc.

Imperfect Subjunctive: *creyera (creyese),* etc.   that I believed/would believe, etc.; if I believed, etc.

Present Perfect Subjunctive: haya creído, etc.   that I (have) believed, etc.

Pluperfect Subjunctive: hubiera (hubiese) creído, etc.   that I had believed/would have believed, etc.; if I had believed, etc.

Additional Note: -er and -ir verbs whose stems end in a vowel have a written accent on the i of the past participle. The past participle of such verbs is otherwise regular. Example: *creer   creído.*

Others:

leer   reír*

poseer   oír*

traer*   huir*

caer*

* See individual conjugations for these verbs *(traer,* pp. 124–125; *caer,* p. 105; *reír,* pp. 94–95; *oír,* p. 116; *huir,* p. 95).

Most verbs ending in *-cer* or *-cir* preceded by a vowel add *z* before *c* when followed by *o* or *a*.

Conocer   to know, be acquainted with

Present Indicative: *conozco,* conoces, etc.   I know, etc.

Imperfect: conocía, etc.   I was knowing, etc.

Preterit: conocí, etc.   I knew, etc.

Future: conoceré, etc.   I will know, etc.

Conditional: conocería, etc.   I would know, etc.

Present Participle: conociendo   knowing

Past Participle: conocido   known

Present Subjunctive: *conozca, conozcas, conozca, conozcamos, conozcáis, conozcan* that I know/will know, etc.

Imperfect Subjunctive: conociera (conociese), etc.   that I knew/would know, etc.; if I knew, etc.

Present Perfect Subjunctive: haya conocido, etc.   that I knew/have known, etc.

Pluperfect Subjunctive: hubiera (hubiese) conocido, etc.   that I had known/would have known, etc.; if I had known, etc.

Others:

agradecer to thank	*desaparecer* to disappear
reconocer to recognize	*enriquecerse* to become rich
desconocer to be unacquainted	*aparecer* to appear
complacer to please	*parecer* to seem
aborrecer to hate	*merecer* to deserve
compadecer to feel sorry for	*obedecer* to obey
carecer to lack	*ofrecer* to offer

Some verbs ending in *-iar* accent the *i* of the stem in all forms of the present indicative and present subjunctive, except the *nosotros* and *vosotros* forms.

Enviar   to send

Present Indicative: *envío, envías, envía,* enviamos, enviáis, *envían*   I send, etc.

Imperfect: enviaba, etc.   I was sending, etc.

Preterit: envié, etc.   I send, etc.

Future: enviaré, etc.   I will send, etc.

Conditional: enviaría, etc.   I would send, etc.

Present Participle: enviando   sending

Past Participle: enviado   sent

Present Subjunctive: *envíe, envíes, envíe,* enviemos, enviéis, *envíen*   that I send/will send, etc.

Imperfect Subjunctive: enviara (enviase), etc.   that I sent/would send, etc.; if I sent, etc.

Present Perfect Subjunctive: haya enviado, etc.   that I (have) sent, etc.

Pluperfect Subjunctive: hubiera (hubiese) enviado, etc.   that I had sent/would have sent, etc.; if I had sent, etc.

Others:

desafiar   to defy, challenge
confiar   to trust
desconfiar   to mistrust
guiar   to guide

Verbs ending in -*uar* preceded by any consonant except *c* or *g* accent the *u* in all forms of the present indicative and present subjunctive except the *nosotros* and *vosotros* forms.

Continuar   to continue

Present Indicative: *continúo, continúas, continúa,* continuamos, continuáis, *continúan*   I continue, etc.
Imperfect: continuaba, etc.   I was continuing, etc.
Preterit: continué, etc.   I continued, etc.
Future: continuaré etc.   I will continue, etc.
Conditional: continuaría, etc.   I would continue, etc.
Present Participle: continuando   continuing
Past Participle: continuado   continued
Present Subjunctive: *continúe, continúes, continúe,* continuemos, continuéis, *continúen*   that I continue/will
              continue, etc.
Imperfect Subjunctive: continuara (continuase), etc.   that I continued/would continue, etc.; if I continued, etc.
Present Perfect Subjunctive: haya continuado, etc.   that I (have) continued, etc.
Pluperfect Subjunctive: hubiera (hubiese) continuado, etc.   that I had continued/would have continued,
              etc.; if I had continued, etc.

Others:
insinuar   to insinuate
habituarse   to grow accustomed to
descontinuar   to discontinue
graduarse   to graduate, be graduated

Para practicar

Write the infinitives in the tense and person indicated:

Present subjunctive   **tú**

aparecer	ofrecer	merecer	reconocer	compadecer	confiar
_____	_____	_____	_____	_____	_____

guiar	descontinuar
_____	_____

Present indicative   **yo**

desafiar	parecer	obedecer	agradecer	insinuar	desconfiar
_____	_____	_____	_____	_____	_____

Preterit   **Uds.**

leer	poseer	enviar	continuar	conocer	ofrecer
_____	_____	_____	_____	_____	_____

Aplicación

Change each verb to the corresponding tense in the plural:

1. estoy leyendo _____
2. envías _____
3. continúes _____
4. ofrezco _____
5. Ud. desafíe _____
6. aborrezcas _____
7. yo merezca _____
8. Ud. aparezca _____
9. guío _____
10. desconoció _____

11. poseyó _____
12. Ud. insinúe _____
13. se enriquezca _____
14. parecí _____
15. me habitué _____
16. yo creyese _____
17. Ud. complacía _____
18. ella desconfía _____
19. descontinúo _____
20. reconozco _____

Mastery Test

Translate into Spanish:

1. did she read? _____
2. it's possible that we will disappear _____
3. I hope she continues _____
4. it's possible that they will send _____
5. I was possessing _____
6. it's possible that you (s., for.) don't know

_____

7. it's possible that we mistrust _____
8. I do not guide _____
9. it is possible that they have read _____

_____

10. it is possible that he feels sorry for _____

11. I was sending _____

12. it's possible that you (s., fam.) will

discontinue _____

13. we were believing _____

14. you (pl., fam.) disappear _____

_____

15. they sent _____

16. she did not believe _____

17. I hated _____

18. do you (s., fam.) trust? _____

_____

19. it's impossible that they know _____

20. she continued _____

17 Orthographic Changes in Stem-Changing Verbs

Verbs ending in *-gar* with stem-vowel *e* or *o* change *g* to *gu* before *e* and also change the stem vowel from *e* to *ie* and *o* to *ue* in all forms of the present indicative and present subjunctive, except the *nosotros* and *vosotros* forms (see pages 69 and 80).

Negar   to deny

Present Indicative: *niego, niegas, niega,* negamos, negáis, *niegan*   I deny, etc.

Preterit: *negué,* negaste, etc.   I denied, etc.

Present Subjunctive: *niegue, niegues, niegue, neguemos, neguéis, nieguen*   that I deny/will deny, etc.

All other forms are regular.

Others:
cegar   to blind
rogar   to ask, beg

Colgar   to hang up

cuelgo, cuelgas, cuelga, colgamos, colgáis, *cuelgan*   I hang up, etc.

colgué, colgaste, etc.   I hung up, etc.

cuelgue, cuelgues, cuelgue, colguemos, colguéis, cuelguen   that I hang up/will hang up, etc.

Note one verb that ends in *-gar* and has the stem vowel *u* change to *ue*, in addition to the orthographic change of *g* to *gu*:

Jugar   to play

Present Indicative: *juego, juegas, juega,* jugamos, jugáis, *juegan*   I play, etc.

Preterit: *jugué,* jugaste, etc.   I played, etc.

Present Subjunctive: *juegue, juegues, juegue, juguemos, juguéis, jueguen*   that I play, will play, etc.

All other forms are regular. Jugar is the only verb of this type.

Verbs ending in *-zar* with the stem vowel *e* or *o* change *z* to *c* before *e* and stem vowels *e* to *ie* and *o* to *ue* in all forms of the present indicative and present subjunctive except the *nosotros* and *vosotros* forms (see pages 62 and 73).

Empezar   to begin

Present Indicative: *empiezo, empiezas, empieza,* empezamos, empezáis, *empiezan*   I begin, etc.

Preterit: *empecé,* empezaste, etc.   I began, etc.

Present Subjunctive: *empiece, empieces, empiece, empecemos, empecéis, empiecen*   that I begin/will begin, etc.

Almorzar   to eat lunch

almuerzo, almuerzas, almuerza, almorzamos, almorzáis, *almuerzan*   I eat lunch, etc.

almorcé, almorzaste, etc.   I ate lunch, etc.

almuerce, almuerces, almuerce, almorcemos, almorcéis, almuercen   that I eat lunch/will eat lunch, etc.

All other forms are regular.

Others:
tropezar   to stumble
esforzarse   to try hard

Verbs ending in *-egir* change *g* to *j* before *o* or *a* and stem-vowel *e* to *i* in accordance with rules for stem-changing verbs of Class III (see pages 77 and 85).

Colegir   to collect
Present Indicative: *colijo, coliges, colige,* colegimos, colegís, *coligen*   I collect, etc.
Preterit: colegí, colegiste, *coligió,* colegimos, colegisteis, *coligieron*   I collected, etc.
Present Participle: *coligiendo*   collecting
Present Subjunctive: *colija, colijas, colija, colijamos, colijáis, colijan*   that I collect/will collect, etc.
Imperfect Subjunctive: *coligiera (coligiese), coligieras, coligiera, coligiéramos, coligierais, coligieran*   that I collected/would collect, etc.; if I collected, etc.

Others:
corregir   to correct
elegir   to elect

Verbs ending in *-eguir* change *gu* to *g* before *o* or *a* and *e* to *i* in accordance with rules for stem-changing verbs of Class III.

Seguir   to follow
Present Indicative: *sigo, sigues, sigue,* seguimos, seguís, *siguen*   I follow, etc.
Preterit: seguí, seguiste, *siguió,* seguimos, seguisteis, *siguieron*   I followed, etc.
Present Participle: *siguiendo*   following
Present Subjunctive: *siga, sigas, siga, sigamos, sigáis, sigan*   that I follow/will follow, etc.
Imperfect Subjunctive: *siguiera* (siguiese), etc.   that I followed/would follow, etc.; if I followed, etc.
Stem has *i* throughout imperfect subjunctive.

Others:
conseguir   to get, obtain
perseguir   to persecute, pursue
proseguir   to prosecute, pursue

Verbs ending in *-eír* change *e* to *i* in accordance with rules of stem-changing verbs of Class III. In addition, when the stem is stressed, the *i* has a written accent. When the stem is not changed and is followed by a stressed *i* in the ending, the *i* requires a written accent, as does the infinitive.

Reír   to laugh
Present Indicative: *río, ríes, ríe,* reímos, reís, *ríen*   I laugh, etc.
Preterit: reí, reíste, *rió,* reímos, reísteis, *rieron*   I laughed, etc.
Present Participle: *riendo*   laughing

Past Participle: reído

Present Subjunctive: *ría, rías, ría, riamos, riáis, rían*   that I laugh/will laugh, etc.

Imperfect Subjunctive: *riera (riese)* etc.   that I laughed/would laugh, etc.; if I laughed, etc.

Others:
sonreír   to smile

Verbs ending in *-uir* insert *y* before all endings after an accented stem and change unaccented *i* to *y* before *e* or *a* in endings (see page 88).

Huir   to flee

Present Indicative: *huyo, huyes, huye,* huímos, huís, *huyen*   I flee, etc.

Preterit: huí, huiste, *huyó,* huimos, huisteis, *huyeron*   I fled, etc.

Present Participle: *huyendo*   fleeing

Present Subjunctive: *huya, huyas, huya, huyamos, huyáis, huyan*   that I run away/will run away, etc.

Imperfect Subjunctive: *huyera (huyese),* etc.   that I ran away/would run away, etc.; if I ran away, etc.

Others:
concluir to conclude	*incluir* to include
destruir to destroy	*restituir* to restore
instruir to instruct	*constituir* to constitute, consist
construir to construct	

Para practicar

Write the verbs in the tense and person indicated:

Present indicative   **yo**

corregir	rogar	cegar	tropezar	conseguir	construir
_____	_____	_____	_____	_____	_____

sonreír

_____

Present indicative Ud.

negar	perseguir	reír	destruir	esforzarse	elegir
_____	_____	_____	_____	_____	_____

jugar

_____

Preterit yo

colegir	rogar	almorzar	incluir	reír	proseguir
_____	_____	_____	_____	_____	_____

cegar

_____

Preterit ellos

corregir	conseguir	sonreír	restituir	elegir	instruir
_____	_____	_____	_____	_____	_____

negar

_____

Present subjunctive tú

cegar	jugar	tropezar	corregir	proseguir	destruir
_____	_____	_____	_____	_____	_____

reír

_____

Present subjunctive nosotros

cegar	esforzarse	elegir	conseguir	sonreír	concluir
_____	_____	_____	_____	_____	_____

jugar

_____

Imperfect subjunctive   **él**

corregir	proseguir	reír	construir	elegir	constituir
_____	_____	_____	_____	_____	_____

conseguir

_____

Present participle

colegir	colgar	almorzar	sonreír	destruir	perseguir
_____	_____	_____	_____	_____	_____

incluir

_____

Past participle

cegar	empezar	elegir	seguir	reír	concluir
_____	_____	_____	_____	_____	_____

huir

_____

Aplicación

Change from singular to plural in the same tense:

1. ruegue Ud. _____

2. tropiezo _____

3. él almuerce _____

4. cegué _____

5. escojo _____

6. empecé _____

7. juega _____

8. me esforcé _____

9. cuelgues _____

10. empiezo _____

11. huye _____

12. Ud. sonrió _____

13. él destruyó _____

14. yo concluyese _____

15. has huido _____

16. él corrija _____

17. Ud. consiguió _____

18. sigo _____

19. yo escogiera _____

20. consigas _____

21. él estaba siguiendo _____

22. yo elija _____

23. corrijo _____

24. persigue _____

25. incluyas _____

26. yo concluía _____

27. Ud. había reído _____

28. instruyo _____

29. Ud. ha restituido _____

30. está sonriendo _____

Mastery Test

Orthographic changes and orthographic-stem changes:

A. Write in English:

1. que yo apague _____

2. ejerzo _____

3. envías _____

4. tropiezo _____

5. ¡extinga Ud.! _____

6. ofrezco _____

7. entregué _____

8. que ellos distingan _____

9. que desconozcas _____

10. jugué _____

11. que finjamos _____

12. guío _____

13. que Ud. almuerce _____

14. corrijo _____

15. él poseyó _____

16. que repliques _____

B. Write in Spanish:

1. I paid _____

2. that I chose _____

3. did she read? _____

4. I did not find out _____

5. they followed _____

6. I hope he continues _____

7. it's possible that he won't place _____

_____

8. it's possible that you (s., fam.) won't extinguish _____

9. I hope that they send _____

10. it's possible that we will arrive _____

_____

11. did you (s., for.) obtain? _____

12. it's possible that you (s., fam.) don't know _____

_____

17. que ellos cojan _____

18. que Ud. insinúe _____

19. amenaces _____

20. exijo _____

21. que yo creyese _____

22. marqué _____

23. que consigas _____

24. sonrío _____

25. que Ud. ruegue _____

26. que ellos convenzan _____

27. que Ud. concluyese _____

28. que Uds. apacigüen _____

29. que delincáis _____

30. destruyó _____

13. it's possible that you will cross _____

_____

14. I follow _____

15. I don't guide _____

16. I begged _____

17. I break the law _____

18. it's possible that you (s., fam.) will read _____

_____

19. I hope that you (pl., fam.) will begin _____

_____

20. it's possible that he will direct _____

_____

21. they destroyed _____

22. I did not explain _____

23. I pretend _____

24. you (s., fam.) do not laugh _____

_____

25. I hope that you will reply _____

_____

26. it's possible that they won't convince _____

_____

27. we were believing _____

28. I threw _____

29. it's possible that you (s., fam.) will choose _____

_____

30. if we concluded _____

Repaso general 1

A. Change each verb from singular to plural in the same tense:

1. parto _____

2. comprendiste _____

3. él vivía _____

4. asistiré _____

5. tomarías _____

6. estoy escribiendo _____

7. estaba vistiéndose _____

8. he hablado _____

9. Ud. había vendido _____

10. habrás asistido _____

11. él habría bebido _____

12. conteste Ud. _____

13. aprendieras _____

14. él haya entrado _____

15. yo hubiera tomado _____

16. acuerdo _____

17. se acueste _____

18. yo consienta _____

19. no se divierte _____

20. Ud. pidió _____

21. leyó _____

22. río _____

23. negué _____

B. Write in Spanish:

1. they fear _____

2. you (s., fam.) used to drink _____
_____

3. I hope you (pl., fam.) show _____
_____

4. I began _____

5. did you (s., fam.) speak? _____
_____

6. they served _____

7. we were believing _____

8. if you (pl., fam.) believed _____
_____

9. he would not write _____

10. he notices _____

11. it's possible that they won't convince _____
_____

12. it's possible that he won't begin _____
_____

13. you (s., fam.) were speaking _____
_____

14. it is snowing _____

15. I hope you (pl., for.) will explain _____
_____

24. Ud. incluya _____

25. juegues _____

26. reconozco _____

27. Ud. persiguió _____

28. almuerces _____

29. averigüe _____

30. distingo _____

16. it's possible that you (pl., for.) will direct _____

_____

17. I will have taught _____

18. if they asked for _____

19. you (s., fam.) do not laugh _____

_____

20. I do not guide _____

21. let us fear _____

22. I choose _____

23. do you (s., fam.) continue? _____

_____

24. I did not explain _____

25. he was selling _____

26. I begged _____

27. they destroyed _____

28. it's possible that you (s., fam.) will choose ____

_____

29. they used to carry _____

30. he sends _____

Repaso general 2

A. Make each simple tense into a compound one in the same person:

1. temía _____

2. parto _____

3. vivían _____

4. necesitaré _____

B. Write in Spanish:

1. they would have left _____

2. I hope they read _____

3. if we concluded _____

4. she is not studying _____

A. Make each simple tense into a compound one in the same person: (*continued*)

5. partiríamos _____

6. comas _____

7. vendiésemos _____

8. Ud. rió _____

9. restituyes _____

10. envían _____

11. descontinúo _____

12. obedezco _____

13. creyó _____

14. desaparezcan _____

15. yo poseyera _____

_____

16. tropieza _____

17. distinga Ud. _____

18. juegan _____

19. expliquen _____

20. consigo _____

21. hirió _____

22. eliges _____

23. él delinca _____

24. sonríen _____

25. destruyeron _____

26. hablaréis _____

B. Write in Spanish: (*continued*)

5. they understand _____

6. I paid _____

7. I hope that you (s., fam.) cross _____

_____

8. you (s., for.) would carry _____

_____

9. it's possible that we will close _____

10. it was possible that I would choose _____

_____

11. did you (s., fam.) obtain? _____

_____

12. it was impossible for us to attend (that we not

attend) _____

13. if you (pl., for.) prevented _____

_____

14. did she read? _____

15. let us arrive _____

16. do you (s., for.) open? _____

17. they prevented _____

_____

18. I did not find out _____

19. you (pl., fam.) do not cross _____

_____

27. aprendí _____

28. durmió _____

29. corrigiéramos _____

30. huyera

20. you (s., fam.) will enter _____
_____

21. I dress myself _____

22. they followed _____

23. I close _____

24. would you (pl., for.) read? _____
_____

25. it's possible that they will die _____

26. continue! (pl., for.) _____

27. I follow _____

28. you (pl., for.) will have lived _____
_____

29. it's possible that you (pl., fam.) will lose _____
_____

30. it's possible that he won't look for _____
_____

18 Irregular Verbs

Andar   to walk

Present Indicative: ando, andas, etc.   I walk, etc.

Imperfect: andaba, etc.   I was walking, etc.

Preterit: *anduve, anduviste, anduvo, anduvimos, anduvisteis, anduvieron*   I walked, etc.

Future: andaré, etc.   I will walk, etc.

Conditional: andaría, etc.   I would walk, etc.

Present Participle: andando   walking

Past Participle: andado   walked

Present Subjunctive: ande, etc.   that I walk/will walk, etc.

Imperfect Subjunctive: *anduviera* (*anduviese*) *anduvieras, anduviera, anduviéramos, anduvierais, anduvieran*   that I walked/would walk, etc.; if I walked, etc.

Present Perfect Subjunctive: haya andado, etc.   that I walked/have walked, etc.

Pluperfect Subjunctive: hubiera (hubiese) andado, etc.   that I had walked/would have walked, etc.; if I had walked, etc.

Asir   to seize

Present Indicative: *asgo*, ases, etc.   I seize, etc.

Imperfect: asía, etc.   I was seizing, etc.

Preterit: así, asiste, etc.   I seized, etc.

Future: asiré, etc.   I will seize, etc.

Conditonal: asiría, etc.   I would seize, etc.

Present Participle: asiendo   seizing

Past Participle: asido   seized

Present Subjunctive: *asga, asgas, asga, asgamos, asgáis, asgan*   that I seize/will sieze, etc.

Imperfect Subjunctive: asiera (asiese), etc.   that I siezed/would sieze, etc.; if I seized, etc.

Present Perfect Subjunctive: haya asido, etc.   that I siezed/have siezed, etc.

Pluperfect Subjunctive: hubiera (hubiese) asido, etc.   that I had siezed/would have siezed, etc.; if I had seized, etc.

Other:
desasir   to loosen

Caber   to be room for, to fit

Present Indicative: *quepo*, cabes, etc.   I fit, etc.

Imperfect: cabía, etc.   I was fitting, etc.

Preterit: *cupe, cupiste, cupo, cupimos, cupisteis, cupieron*   I fitted, etc.

Future: *cabré, cabrás, cabrá, cabremos, cabréis, cabrán*   I will fit, etc.

Conditional: *cabría,* etc.   I would fit, etc.

Present Participle: cabiendo   fitting

Past Participle: cabido   fitted

Present Subjunctive: *quepa, quepas, quepa, quepamos, quepáis, quepan*   that I fit/will fit, etc.

Imperfect Subjunctive: *cupiera* (*cupiese*), etc.   that I fit/would fit, etc.; if I fit, etc.

Present Perfect Subjunctive: haya cabido, etc.   that I fit/have fit, etc.

Pluperfect Subjunctive: hubiera (hubiese) cabido, etc.   that I had fit/would have fit, etc.; if I had fit, etc.

Caer   to fall

Present Indicative: *caigo,* caes, cae, caemos, caéis, caen   I fall, etc.

Imperfect: caía, etc.   I was falling, etc.

Preterit: caí, caíste, *cayó,* caímos, caísteis, *cayeron*   I fell, etc.

Future: caeré, etc.   I will fall, etc.

Conditional: caería, etc.   I would fall, etc.

Present Participle: *cayendo*   falling

Past Participle: caído   fallen

Present Subjunctive: *caiga, caigas, caiga, caigamos, caigáis, caigan*   that I fall/will fall, etc.

Imperfect Subjunctive: *cayera,* (*cayese*), etc.   that I fell/would fall, etc., if I fell, etc.

Present Perfect Subjunctive: haya caído, etc.   that I fell/have fallen, etc.

Pluperfect Subjunctive: hubiera (hubiese) caído, etc.   that I had fallen/would have fallen, etc.;
                    if I had fallen, etc.

Others:
decaer   to decline, decay, fade

Para practicar

Write the verbs in the tense and person indicated:

Present indicative   **yo**

desasir	caber	andar	decaer
_____	_____	_____	_____

Uds.

asir	andar	caer	caber
_____	_____	_____	_____

Preterit   **él**

desasir	caber	andar	caer
_____	_____	_____	_____

Future **nosotros**

asir   decaer   caber   andar

_____   _____   _____   _____

Present subjunctive **tú**

desasir   caer   caber   andar

_____   _____   _____   _____

Imperfect subjunctive **vosotros**

decaer   andar   caber   asir

_____   _____   _____   _____

Aplicación

Translate into English:

1. ellos caerían _____

2. cabremos _____

3. que hayas caído _____

4. andabais _____

5. Uds. cabrían _____

6. ellos cayeron _____

7. decaeríais _____

8. cupiste _____

9. desasimos _____

10. anduvimos _____

11. que decaigamos _____

12. que ellos quepan _____

13. que Uds. caigan _____

14. asiré _____

15. decaímos _____

16. él caerá _____

17. que yo cupiera _____

18. caigo _____

19. quepo _____

20. que ellos asgan _____

21. que decayeras _____

22. andaremos _____

23. que ellos hubieran asido _____

24. ellos habrían andado _____

25. Uds. desasirán _____

26. ellos están decayendo _____

27. que andemos _____

28. él habrá decaído _____

29. que ellos anduviesen _____

30. Uds. asen _____

Mastery Test

Write in Spanish:

1. that they would not fall _____

2. that I had walked _____

3. they would seize _____

4. were you (s., fam.) walking? _____

_____

5. they are fading _____

6. if they loosened _____

7. that you (pl., fam.) would decline _____

_____

8. will I walk? _____

9. I loosen _____

10. he walked _____

11. did he fit? _____

12. we were loosening _____

13. they declined _____

14. we should have fitted _____

_____

15. I will not fall _____

16. he fits _____

17. I hope we walk _____

18. he had seized _____

19. he would not have fallen _____

_____

20. he may walk _____

21. you (s., fam.) had seized _____

_____

22. I walk _____

23. you (pl., for.) would fall _____

_____

24. did he seize? _____

25. he has fallen _____

26. I hope we fit _____

27. you (s., fam.) used to walk _____

_____

28. we were falling _____

29. that you (s., fam.) have walked _____

_____

30. we had fitted _____

31. that I have seized _____

32. you (pl., fam.) fell _____

33. if I had fallen _____

34. you (s., for.) fitted _____

108

35. if I fit _____

36. you (s., fam.) decline _____

37. that they seize _____

38. if we fell _____

39. it's possible that I won't fit _____

40. that you (pl., for.) will fall _____

_____

Conducir   to drive, lead, conduct

Present Indicative: *conduzco*, conduces, etc.   I drive, etc.

Imperfect: conducía, etc.   I was driving, etc.

Preterit: *conduje, condujiste, condujo, condujimos, condujisteis, condujeron*   I drove, etc.

Future: conduciré, etc.   I will drive, etc.

Conditional: conduciría, etc.   I would drive, etc.

Present Participle: conduciendo   driving

Past Participle: conducido   drove

Present Subjunctive: *conduzca, conduzcas, conduzca, conduzcamos, conduzcáis, conduzcan*
              that I drive/will drive, etc.

Imperfect Subjunctive: *condujera* (*condujese*), etc.   that I drove/would drive, etc.; if I drove, etc.

Present Perfect Subjunctive: haya conducido, etc.   that I drove/have driven, etc.

Pluperféct Subjunctive: hubiera (hubiese) conducido, etc.   that I had driven/would have driven, etc.;
              if I had driven, etc.

Others:
deducir   to deduce
traducir   to translate
producir   to produce

Dar   to give

Present Indicative: *doy,* das, da, damos, *dais,* dan   I give, etc.

Imperfect: daba, etc.   I was giving, etc.

Preterit: *di, diste, dio, dimos, disteis, dieron*   I gave, etc.

Future: daré, etc.   I will give, etc.

Conditional: daría, etc.   I would give, etc.

Present Participle: dando   giving

Past Participle: dado   given

Present Sujunctive: *dé, des, dé, demos, deis, den*   that I give/will give, etc.

Imperfect Subjunctive: *diera*, (*diese*), etc.   that I gave/would give, etc.; if I gave, etc.

Present Perfect Subjunctive: haya dado, etc.   that I gave/have given, etc.

Pluperfect Subjunctive: hubiera (hubiese) dado, etc.   that I had given/would have given, etc.;
      if I had given, etc.

Decir   to say, tell

Present Indicative: *digo, dices, dice,* decimos, decís, *dicen*   to say, etc.

Imperfect: decía, etc.   I was saying, etc.

Preterit: *dije, dijiste, dijo, dijimos, dijisteis, dijeron*   I said, etc.

Future: *diré, dirás, dirá, diremos, diréis, dirán*   I will tell, etc.

Conditional: *diría,* etc.   I would tell, etc.

Present Participle: *diciendo*   saying

Past Participle: *dicho*   said

Present Subjunctive: *diga, digas, diga, digamos, digáis, digan*   that I say/will say, etc.

Imperfect Subjunctive: *dijera* (*dijese*), etc.   that I said/would say, etc.; if I said, etc.

Present Perfect Subjunctive: haya *dicho*, etc.   that I said/have said, etc.

Pluperfect Subjunctive: hubiera (hubiese) *dicho,* etc.   that I had said/would have said, etc.; if I had said, etc.

Others:
maldecir   to curse
bendecir   to bless*

* Note that *maldecir* and *bendecir* are regular in the future and the conditional (*maldeciré, bendeciría,* etc.). The past participles of these verbs are also regular (*maldecido, bendecido*).

Errar   to err, to wander

Pesent Indicative: *yerro, yerras, yerra,* erramos, erráis, *yerran*   I wander, etc.

Imperfect: erraba, etc.   I was wandering, etc.

Preterit: erré, etc.   I wandered, etc.

Future: erraré, etc.   I will wander, etc.

Conditional: erraría, etc.   I would wander, etc.

Present participle: errando   wandering

Past Participle: errado   wandered

Present Subjunctive: *yerre, yerres, yerre,* erremos, erréis, *yerren*   that I err/will err, etc.

Imperfect Subjunctive: errara (errase), etc.   that I erred/would err, etc.; if I erred, etc.

Present Perfect Subjunctive: haya errado, etc.   that I erred/have erred, etc.

Pluperfect Subjunctive: hubiera (hubiese) errado, etc.   that I had erred/would have erred, etc.;
      if I had erred, etc.

Para practicar

Write the verbs in the person and tense indicated:

Present indicative **yo**

deducir	maldecir	errar	dar	traducir
_____	_____	_____	_____	_____

Preterit **ellos**

producir	bendecir	dar	conducir	errar
_____	_____	_____	_____	_____

Future **Ud.**

traducir	maldecir	deducir	bendecir	dar
_____	_____	_____	_____	_____

Pluperfect indicative **Uds.**

dar	deducir	bendecir	errar	decir
_____	_____	_____	_____	_____

Present subjunctive **tú**

dar	producir	bendecir	errar	decir
_____	_____	_____	_____	_____

Imperfect subjunctive **nosotros**

errar	traducir	maldecir	dar	conducir
_____	_____	_____	_____	_____

Aplicación

Write in English:

1. dedujisteis _____

2. das _____

3. él dirá _____

4. que erremos _____

5. conducíamos _____

6. que ellos den _____

7. que digamos _____

8. maldecías _____

9. él traduce _____

10. Ud. habría dado _____

11. ellos dijeron _____

12. que yo haya dicho _____

13. ella condujo _____

14. doy _____

15. yerres _____

16. diríamos _____

17. que yo deduzca _____

18. Ud. dio _____

19. ellos bendicen _____

20. Uds. yerran _____

21. él produciría _____

22. que dieras _____

23. que él dijera _____

24. yerro _____

25. que ella tradujera _____

26. dábamos _____

27. ellos habrían maldicho _____

_____

28. erré _____

29. produzco _____

30. daré _____

Mastery Test

Write in Spanish:

1. you (s., fam.) will say _____

_____

2. you (pl., fam.) lead _____

3. let us wander _____

4. it's possible that she told _____

5. he was not giving _____

6. you (s., fam.) translated _____

_____

7. if he blessed _____

8. we will give _____

9. it's impossible for you (pl., for.) to produce

_____

10. did he lead? _____

11. if you (s., fam.) had said _____

_____

12. does he give? _____

13. I do wander _____

14. it's possible that he will deduce _____

15. we would curse _____

16. they gave _____

17. if I produced _____

18. do not translate! (pl., for.) _____

19. are they saying? _____

20. they wandered _____

21. it's possible that they have given _____

_____

22. have you (pl., fam.) not told? _____

_____

23. I produce _____

24. he wanders _____

25. we will not tell _____

26. they were not saying _____

27. I do not give _____

28. it's possible that I will deduce _____

29. if they didn't translate _____

_____

30. you (s., fam.) cursed _____

31. did you (pl., fam.) give? _____

_____

32. we will lead _____

33. I hope you (s., for.) give _____

_____

34. I bless _____

35. they produced _____

36. you (s., fam.) were translating _____

_____

37. it's possible that he didn't give _____

38. it's possible that he will curse _____

39. if they hadn't given _____

40. it's possible that he won't drive _____

Estar   to be (in a state or condition)

Present Indicative: *estoy, estás, está,* estamos, estáis, *están*   I am, etc.

Imperfect: estaba, etc.   I was, etc.

Preterit: *estuve, estuviste, estuvo, estuvimos, estuvisteis, estuvieron*   I was, etc.

Future: estaré, etc.   I will be, etc.

Conditional: estaría, etc.   I would be, etc.

Present Participle: estando   being

Past Participle: estado   been

Present Subjunctive: *esté, estés, esté,* estemos, estéis, *estén*   that I will be etc.

Imperfect Subjunctive: *estuviera* (*estuviese*), etc.   that I was/would be, etc.; if I were, etc.

Present Perfect Subjunctive: haya estado, etc.   that I was/have been, etc.

Pluperfect Subjunctive: hubiera (hubiese) estado, etc.   that I had been/would have been, etc.; if I had been

Haber   to have (used only as an auxiliary with perfect tenses or in idiomatic expressions. Some tenses are defective, i.e., they do not have complete forms)

Present Indicative: *he, has, ha, hemos,* habéis, *han*   I have, etc.; *hay*   there is, are

Imperfect: había, etc.   I had, etc.; había   there was, were

Preterit: *hube,* hubiste, *hubo, hubimos, hubisteis, hubieron*   I had, etc.; *hubo*   there was, were

Future: *habré, habrás, habrá, habremos, habréis, habrán.*   I will have, etc.; *habrá*   there will be

Conditional: *habría, etc.*   I would have, etc.; *habría*   there would be

Present Participle: habiendo   having, there being

Past Participle: habido   ha (había, habrá, habría) habido   there has (had, will have, would have) been

Present Subjunctive: *haya, hayas, haya, hayamos, hayáis, hayan*   I may have, etc. *haya*   that I will have ___, etc./there are/will be'

Imperfect Subjunctive: *hubiera (hubiese), etc.*   I might have, etc.; *hubiera (hubiese)* that I had ___/would have ___, etc., there were'; if I had ____, etc.

Present Perfect Subjunctive: haya habido   that there were/have been'

Pluperfect Subjunctive: hubiera (hubiese) habido   that there had been; if there had been

Hacer   to do, make

Present Indicative: *hago,* haces, hace, hacemos, hacéis, hacen   I do, etc.

Imperfect: hacía, etc.   I was doing, etc.

Preterit: *hice, hiciste, hizo, hicimos, hicisteis, hicieron*   I did, etc.

Future: *haré, harás, hará, haremos, haréis, harán*   I will do, etc.

Conditional: *haría,* etc.   I would do, etc.

Present Participle: haciendo   doing

Past Participle: *hecho*   done

Present Subjunctive: *haga, hagas, haga, hagamos, hagáis, hagan*   that I do/will do, etc.

Imperfect Subjunctive: *hiciera (hiciese),* etc.   that I did/would do, etc.; if I did, etc.

Present Perfect Subjunctive: haya *hecho,* etc.   that I did/have done, etc.

Pluperfect Subjunctive: hubiera (hubiese) *hecho,* etc.   that I had done/would have done, etc.; if I had done, etc.

Other:
satisfacer   to satisfy

Ir   to go

Present Indicative: *voy, vas, va, vamos, vais, van*   I go, etc.

Imperfect: *iba, ibas, iba, íbamos, ibais, iban*   I was going, etc.

Preterit: *fui, fuiste, fue, fuimos, fuisteis, fueron*   I went, etc.

Future: iré, etc.   I will go, etc.

Conditional: iría, etc.   I would go, etc.

Present Participle: *yendo*   going

Past Participle: ido   gone

Present Subjunctive: *vaya, vayas, vaya, vayamos, vayáis, vayan*   that I go/will go, etc.

Imperfect Subjunctive: *fuera* (*fuese*), etc.   that I went/would go, etc.; if I went, etc.

Present Perfect Subjunctive: haya ido, etc.   that I went/have gone, etc.

Pluperfect Subjunctive: hubiera (hubiese) ido, etc.   that I had gone/would have gone, etc.; if I had gone, etc.

Para practicar

Change to the plural of the same tense:

1. voy _____

2. Ud. satisfaga _____

3. habrá _____

4. estoy _____

5. ibas _____

6. yo hubiera _____

7. he _____

8. estuvo _____

9. fui _____

10. hará _____

11. hubiste _____

12. hicieras _____

13. él vaya _____

14. estuvieras _____

15. has hecho _____

16. Ud. haya _____

17. fueras _____

18. satisfizo _____

19. Ud. esté _____

20. satisfago _____

Aplicación

Translate into English:

1. él habrá satisfecho _____

2. estamos _____

3. hay _____

4. fuiste _____

5. él haría _____

6. satisficiste _____

7. habría habido _____

8. que hayas hecho _____

9. yo no estaría _____

10. satisfaré _____

11. ellos habían _____

12. hacíamos _____

13. ibais _____

14. que satisficiésemos _____

15. que haya habido _____

16. yo habría estado _____

17. que Ud. satisfaga _____

18. que estuvieras _____

19. habrías _____

20. hicimos _____

21. ellos estaban _____

22. que él hiciera _____

23. él ha _____

24. que no vayas _____

25. yo habría hecho _____

26. satisfacías _____

27. que fuéramos _____

28. que estén _____

29. estuve _____

30. va _____

Mastery Test

Write in Spanish:

1. that we had gone _____

2. I was (pret) _____

3. that I have done _____

4. they would have satisfied _____

_____

5. he was (imperfect) _____

6. they will not have gone _____

_____

7. we were not doing _____

8. you (pl., for.) will satisfy _____

_____

9. we are _____

10. I had done _____

11. he was going _____

12. I satisfied _____

13. I hope we are _____

14. there are not _____

15. we do not satisfy _____

16. does she go? _____

17. you (s., for.) will be _____

18. they did _____

19. I hope we satisfy _____

20. it's possible that I wasn't _____

21. there would have been _____

_____

22. if you (s., fam.) went _____

_____

23. he was satisfying _____

24. there will be _____

25. it's possible that I will go _____

26. if there were _____

27. it's impossible that he will satisfy _____

_____

28. you (s., fam.) will do _____

_____

29. if there were _____

30. if they had been _____

_____

31. you (pl., fam.) went _____

32. there has been _____

33. I hope they don't do _____

34. I satisfy _____

35. if they hadn't done _____

36. I will not go _____

37. I hope there will be _____

38. we would do _____

39. there was (imperfect) _____

40. I am not _____

Oír   to hear

Present Indicative: *oigo, oyes, oye,* oímos, oís, *oyen*   I hear, etc.

Imperfect: oía, oías, etc.   I was hearing, etc.

Preterit: oí, oíste, *oyó,* oímos, oísteis, *oyeron*   I heard, etc.

Future: oiré, etc.   I will hear, etc.

Conditional: oiría, etc.   I would hear, etc.

Present Participle: *oyendo*   hearing

Past Participle: oído   heard

Present Subjunctive: *oiga, oigas, oiga, oigamos, oigáis, oigan*   that I hear/will hear, etc.

Imperfect Subjunctive: *oyera* (*oyese*), etc.   that I heard/would hear etc.; if I heard, etc.

Present Perfect Subjunctive: haya oído, etc.   that I heard/have heard, etc.

Pluperfect Subjunctive: hubiera (hubiese) oído, etc.   that I had heard/would have heard, etc.;
                if I had heard, etc.

Oler   to smell

Present Indicative: *huelo, hueles, huele,* olemos, oléis, *huelen*   I smell, etc.

Imperfect: olía, etc.   I was smelling, etc.

Preterit: olí, oliste, etc.   I smelled, etc.

Future: oleré, etc.   I will smell, etc.

Conditional: olería, etc.   I would smell, etc.

Present Participle: oliendo   smelling

Past Participle: olido   smelled

Present Subjunctive: *huela, huelas, huela,* olamos, oláis, *huelan*   that I smell/will smell, etc.

Imperfect Subjunctive: oliera (oliese), etc.   that I smelled/would smell, etc.; if I smelled, etc.

Present Perfect Subjunctive: haya olido, etc.   that I smelled/have smelled, etc.

Pluperfect Subjunctive: hubiera (hubiese) olido, etc.   that I had smelled/would have smelled, etc.; if I had smelled, etc.

Poder   to be able

Present Indicative: *puedo, puedes, puede,* podemos, podéis, *pueden*   I can, am able, etc.

Imperfect: podía, etc.   I was able, could, etc.

Preterit: *pude, pudiste, pudo, pudimos, pudisteis, pudieron*   I was able, could, etc.

Future: *podré, podrás, podra, podremos, podréis, podrán*   I will be able, etc.

Conditional: *podría,* etc.   I would be able, could, etc.

Present Participle: *pudiendo*   being able

Past Participle: podido   been able

Present Subjunctive: *pueda, puedas, pueda,* podamos, podáis, *puedan*   that I can/will be able, etc.

Imperfect Subjunctive: *pudiera* (*pudiese*), etc.   that I could/would be able, etc.; if I were able, etc.

Present Perfect Subjunctive: haya podido, etc.   that I could/have been able, etc.

Pluperfect Subjunctive: hubiera (hubiese) podido, etc.   that I had been able/would have been able, etc.; if I had been able, etc.

Poner   to put, place

Present Indicative: *pongo,* pones, pone, ponemos, ponéis, ponen   I put, etc.

Imperfect: ponía, etc.   I was putting, etc.

Preterit: puse, *pusiste, puso, pusimos, pusisteis, pusieron*   I put, did put, etc.

Future: *pondré, pondrás, pondrá, pondremos, pondréis, pondrán*   I will put, etc.

Conditional: *pondría,* etc.   I would put, etc.

Present Participle: poniendo   putting

Past Participle: *puesto*   put

Present Subjunctive: *ponga, pongas, ponga, pongamos, pongáis, pongan*   that I put/will put, etc.

Imperfect Subjunctive: *pusiera* (*pusiese*), etc.   that I put/would put, etc.; if I put, etc.

Present Perfect Subjunctive: haya *puesto,* etc.   that I put/have put, etc.

Pluperfect Subjunctive: hubiera (hubiese) *puesto,* etc.   that I had put/would have put, etc.; if I had put, etc.

Others:

disponer to dispose	*imponer* to impose
exponer to expose	*proponer* to propose
componer to compose	*suponer* to suppose

Para practicar

Change the verbs to the tense and person indicated:

Present indicative **tú**

proponer	oler	poder	oír	componer
_____	_____	_____	_____	_____

Preterit **Uds.**

disponer	poder	oír	imponer	suponer
_____	_____	_____	_____	_____

Future **yo**

disponer	exponer	imponer	proponer	suponer
_____	_____	_____	_____	_____

Present subjunctive **él**

componer	poder	oír	oler	exponer
_____	_____	_____	_____	_____

Present perfect subjunctive **nosotros**

oír	disponer	poner	suponer	poder
_____	_____	_____	_____	_____

Aplicación

Change the singular verb to plural, retaining the same tense:

1. él pusiera _____
2. yo pueda _____
3. él oiría _____
4. pudiste _____
5. dispones _____
6. yo oía _____
7. Ud. podrá _____
8. olió _____

9. he compuesto _____
10. habré podido _____
11. oiré _____
12. olerías _____
13. él impondría _____
14. él podía _____
15. habrá oído _____
16. huele _____

17. yo exponga _____

18. oyó _____

19. yo pudiera _____

20. yo haya propuesto _____

21. podrías _____

22. oigas _____

23. huelo _____

24. supondrás _____

25. puedes _____

26. Ud. oye _____

27. huelas _____

28. dispuso _____

29. yo oliera _____

30. hubieras puesto _____

Mastery Test

Write in Spanish:

1. you (s., fam.) heard _____

_____

2. we had not been able _____

_____

3. it's possible that it will smell _____

4. I would not have put _____

5. you (pl., fam.) were not hearing _____

_____

6. they are imposing _____

7. I was able _____

8. does he smell? _____

9. they would hear _____

10. he may be able _____

11. I will have composed _____

_____

12. does she put? _____

13. does he hear? _____

14. you (s., fam.) will not expose _____

_____

15. I hope they propose _____

16. I might not be able _____

17. it was possible that we heard _____

18. you (pl., for.) would be able _____

19. it was impossible that they smelled _____

_____

20. it's possible that we suppose _____

_____

21. you (pl., fam.) will not hear _____

22. are you (s., fam.) able? _____

_____

23. if we disposed _____

24. they will not put _____

25. they heard _____

26. you (pl., fam.) were able (pret) _____

_____

27. she was supposing _____

28. you (s., fam.) will be able _____

_____

29. if we didn't hear _____

30. did you (pl., fam.) expose? _____

_____

Querer   to want, wish, love

Present Indicative: *quiero, quieres, quiere,* queremos, queréis, *quieren*   I want, etc.

Imperfect: quería, etc.   I was wishing, etc.

Preterit: *quise, quisiste, quiso, quisimos, quisisteis, quisieron*   I wanted, etc.

Future: *querré, querrás, querrá, querremos, querréis, querrán*   I shall want, etc.

Conditional: *querría,* etc.   I would wish, etc.

Present Participle: queriendo   wanting

Past Participle: querido   wanted

Present Subjunctive: *quiera, quieras, quiera,* queramos, queráis, *quieran*   that I want/will want, etc.

Imperfect Subjunctive: *quisiera* (*quisiese*), etc.   that I wanted/would want, etc.; if I wanted, etc.

Present Perfect Subjunctive: haya querido, etc.   that I wanted/have wanted, etc.

Pluperfect Subjunctive: hubiera (hubiese) querido, etc.   that I had wanted/would have wanted, etc.;
        if I had wanted, etc.

Saber   to know (a fact)

Present Indicative: *sé,* sabes, sabe, sabemos, sabéis, saben   I know, etc.

Imperfect: sabía, etc.   I was knowing, etc.

Preterit: *supe, supiste, supo, supimos, supisteis, supieron*   I knew, found out, etc.

Future: *sabré, sabrás, sabrá, sabremos, sabréis, sabrán*   I will know, etc.

Conditional: *sabría,* etc.   I would know, etc.

Present Participle: sabiendo   knowing

Past Participle: sabido   known

Present Subjunctive: *sepa, sepas, sepa, sepamos, sepáis, sepan*   that I know/will know, etc.

Imperfect Subjunctive: *supiera* (*supiese*), etc.   that I knew/would know, etc.; if I knew, etc.

Present Perfect Subjunctive: haya sabido, etc.   that I knew/have known, etc.

Pluperfect Subjunctive: hubiera (hubiese) sabido, etc.   that I had known/would have known, etc.;
        if I had known

Salir   to go out, leave

Present Indicative: *salgo,* sales, sale, salimos, salís, salen   I go out, etc.

Imperfect: salía, etc.   I was going out, etc.

Preterit: salí, etc.   I went out, etc.

Future: *saldré, saldrás, saldrá, saldremos, saldréis, saldrán*   I will go out, etc.

Conditional: *saldría, etc.*   I would go out, etc.

Present Participle: saliendo   going out

Past Participle: salido   gone out

Present Subjunctive: *salga, salgas, salga, salgamos, salgáis, salgan*   that I go out/will go out, etc.

Imperfect Subjunctive: saliera (saliese), etc.   that I went out/would go out, etc.; if I went out, etc.

Present Perfect Subjunctive: haya salido, etc.   that I went out/have gone out, etc.

Pluperfect Subjunctive: hubiera (hubiese) salido, etc.   that I had gone out/would have gone out, etc.; if I had gone out

Ser   to be

Present Indicative: *soy, eres, es, somos, sois, son*   I am, etc.

Imperfect: *era, eras, era, éramos, erais, eran*   I was, etc.

Preterit: *fui, fuiste, fue, fuimos, fuisteis, fueron*   I was, etc.

Future: seré, etc.   I will be, etc.

Conditional: sería, etc.   I would be, etc.

Present Participle: siendo   being

Past Participle: sido   been

Present Subjunctive: *sea, seas, sea, seamos, seáis, sean*   that I am/will be, etc.

Imperfect Subjunctive: *fuera (fuese),* etc.   that I was/would be, etc.; if I were, etc.

Present Perfect Subjunctive: haya sido, etc.   that I was/have been, etc.

Pluperfect Subjuctive: hubiera (hubiese) sido, etc.   that I had been/would have been, etc.; if I had been, etc.

Note: The preterits of *ser* and *ir* are identical. The context makes clear which one is intended.

122

Aplicación

A. Change each verb to express past time in the same person.

1. somos _____
2. sepas _____
3. salimos _____
4. sabe _____
5. eres _____
6. salga _____
7. él sea _____
8. soy _____
9. queremos _____
10. salgo _____
11. he sabido _____
12. habéis salido _____
13. quiere _____
14. estás saliendo _____
15. quieran _____

B. Change each singular verb to plural in the same tense.

1. yo salía _____
2. Ud. sabrá _____
3. tú querrás _____
4. salió _____
5. sepas _____
6. saldrías _____
7. sabe _____
8. eres _____
9. yo había querido _____
10. salga _____
11. será _____
12. él quisiera _____
13. saldré _____
14. yo sea _____
15. Ud. fuera _____

C. Translate into English:

1. seríamos _____
2. fuimos _____
3. quisiste _____
4. habré sido _____
5. que fueses _____
6. he sabido _____
7. habremos sabido _____
8. que queramos _____
9. sabréis _____
10. erais _____

11. él supo _____

12. él había salido _____

13. ellos querían _____

14. sabríais _____

15. que hayan salido _____

16. si hubiéramos sabido _____

17. que yo sea _____

18. si él quisiera _____

19. salieran _____

20. si supiéramos _____

Mastery Test

Write in Spanish:

1. if he knew _____

2. you (pl., fam.) have gone out _____

_____

3. he would want _____

4. I was not (pret) _____

5. you (pl., fam.) have known _____

_____

6. we are _____

7. I hope he goes out _____

_____

8. you (s., fam.) will want _____

9. we were knowing _____

10. he was (imperf.) _____

11. we were wanting _____

12. it's possible that we won't go out _____

13. you (pl., fam.) will know _____

_____

14. I hope they are _____

15. it's possible that I have wanted _____

16. you (s., for.) will not be _____

_____

17. they will have known _____

18. they went out _____

19. you (s., fam.) had wanted _____

_____

20. we are not going out _____

21. it's possible that he knew _____

22. is he? _____

23. you (s., fam.) used to go out _____

_____

24. I did not want _____

25. they would have known _____

_____

26. don't they want? _____

27. we have been _____

_____

28. he will go out _____

29. we should know _____

30. if you (pl., for.) wanted _____

31. I am going out _____

32. you (s., for.) knew _____

33. I have wanted _____

34. it's possible that we were _____

35. it's possible that you (s., fam.) (will) want _____

_____

36. would they go out? _____

37. I know _____

38. if he were _____

39. they were (pret.) _____

40. we will have been _____

Tener   to have, hold, possess

Present Indicative: *tengo, tienes, tiene,* tenemos, tenéis, *tienen*   I have, etc.

Imperfect: tenía, etc.   I was having, etc.

Preterit: *tuve, tuviste, tuvo, tuvimos, tuvisteis, tuvieron*   I had, etc.

Future: *tendré, tendrás, tendrá, tendremos, tendréis, tendrán*   I will have, etc.

Conditional: *tendría*, etc.   I would have, etc.

Present Participle: teniendo   having

Past Participle: tenido   had

Present Subjunctive: *tenga, tengas, tenga, tengamos, tengáis, tengan*   that I have/will have, etc.

Imperfect Subjunctive: *tuviera* (*tuviese*), etc.   that I had/would have, etc.; if I had, etc.

Present Perfect Subjunctive: haya tenido, etc.   that I had/have had, etc.

Pluperfect Subjunctive: hubiera (hubiese) tenido, etc.   that I had had/would have had, etc.; if I had had

Others:

contener   to contain

detener   to stop

mantener   to maintain

retener   to retain

sostener   to sustain

Traer   to bring

Present Indicative: *traigo,* traes, trae, etc.   I bring, etc.

Imperfect: traía, etc.   I was bringing, etc.

Preterit: *traje, trajiste, trajo, trajimos, trajisteis, trajeron*   I brought, etc.

Future: traeré, etc.   I will bring, etc.

Conditional: traería, etc.   I would bring, etc.

Present Participle: *trayendo*   bringing

Past Participle: traído   brought

Present Subjunctive: *traiga, traigas, traiga, traigamos, traigáis, traigan*   that I bring/will bring, etc.

Imperfect Subjunctive: *trajera (trajese)*, etc.   that I brought/would bring, etc.; if I brought, etc.

Present Perfect Subjunctive: haya traído, etc.   that I brought/have brought, etc.

Pluperfect Subjunctive: hubiera (hubiese) traído, etc.   that I had brought/would have brought, etc.; if I had brought, etc.

Others:

contraer   to contract

Valer   to be worth

Present Indicative: *valgo,* vales, vale, valemos, valéis, valen   I am worth, etc.

Imperfect: valía, etc.   I was worth, etc.

Preterit: valí, valiste, etc.   I was worth

Future: *valdré, valdrás, valdrá, valdremos, valdréis, valdrán*   I will be worth

Conditional: *valdría*, etc.   I would be worth, etc.

Present Participle: valiendo   being worth

Past Participle: valido   valued

Present Subjunctive: *valga, valgas, valga, valgamos, valgáis, valgan*   that I am worth/will be worth, etc.

Imperfect Subjunctive: valiera (valiese), etc.   that I was worth/would be worth, etc.; if I were worth, etc.

Present Perfect Subjunctive: haya valido, etc.   that I was worth/have been worth, etc.

Pluperfect Subjunctive: hubiera (hubiese) valido, etc.   that I had been worth/would have been worth, etc.; if I had been worth, etc.

Venir   to come

Present Indicative: *vengo, vienes, viene,* venimos, venís, *vienen*   I come, etc.

Imperfect: venía, etc.   I was coming, etc.

Preterit: *vine, viniste, vino, vinimos, vinisteis, vinieron*   I came, etc.

Future: *vendré, vendrás, vendrá, vendremos, vendréis, vendrán*   I will come, etc.

Conditional: *vendría*, etc.   I would come, etc.

Present Participle: viniendo   coming

Past Participle: venido   come

Present Subjunctive: *venga, vengas, venga, vengamos, vengáis, vengan*   that I come/will come, etc.

Imperfect Subjunctive: *viniera* (*viniese*) etc.   that I came/would come, etc.; if I came, etc.

Present Perfect Subjunctive: haya venido, etc.   that I came/have come, etc.

Pluperfect Subjunctive: hubiera (hubiese) venido, etc.   that I had come/would have come, etc.;
if I had come, etc.

Others:

convenir   to be suitable, agree

Para practicar

Change the verbs to the tense and person indicated:

Present indicative   **yo**

contraer	convenir	detener	mantener	sostener
_____	_____	_____	_____	_____

Present indicative   **Ud.**

mantener	venir	valer	retener	traer
_____	_____	_____	_____	_____

Future   **ellos**

convenir	detener	mantener	valer	sostener
_____	_____	_____	_____	_____

Preterit   **él**

contener	traer	convenir	sostener	detener
_____	_____	_____	_____	_____

Present subjunctive   **tú**

venir	mantener	contraer	contener	valer
_____	_____	_____	_____	_____

Imperfect subjunctive   **nosotros**

contraer	venir	tener	sostener	mantener
_____	_____	_____	_____	_____

Aplicación

Write in English:

1. él habrá venido _____
2. que hayas traído _____
3. ellas tuvieron _____
4. que valgamos _____
5. ellos traerán _____
6. tuve _____
7. valdríamos _____
8. ellas habían venido _____
9. teníamos _____
10. traerías _____
11. has valido _____
12. vienes _____
13. valdrás _____
14. si él viniera _____
15. traje _____

16. tendré _____
17. si él valiera _____
18. que ellos tuvieran _____
19. él ha traído _____
20. que ellos vengan _____
21. ellos traían _____
22. Ud. tendría _____
23. valíamos _____
24. habremos venido _____
25. que traigas _____
26. Uds. tienen _____
27. yo valdría _____
28. si tuvieras _____
29. que trajéramos _____
30. venías _____

Mastery Test

Write in Spanish:

1. she has not come _____
2. he had had _____
3. I hope you (s., fam.) bring _____
4. he was worth (pret) _____
5. it's possible that we had _____
6. they had brought _____

7. you (pl., fam.) came _____
8. he used to bring _____
9. he had _____
10. they are worth _____
11. they would not have _____
12. she brought _____

13. they were coming _____

14. do you (s., fam.) have? _____

15. I hope they bring _____

16. it's possible that he will come _____

17. we are not bringing _____

18. we will have _____

19. you (s., fam.) will be worth _____

20. do you (pl., fam.) have? _____

21. I hope you (s., fam.) don't bring _____
_____

22. I am coming _____

23. it's possible that you (pl., for.) have _____
_____

24. I am not worth _____

25. it's impossible that you (s., fam.) have come
_____

26. he would not bring _____

27. they had _____

28. they brought _____

29. will they come? _____

30. it was possible that you (pl., fam.) had _____
_____

31. if he were worth _____

32. you (s., fam.) used to have _____

33. let us bring _____

34. he has had _____

35. you (s., fam.) have brought _____

36. didn't they have? _____

37. it would not be worth _____

38. you (pl., fam.) are bringing _____

39. it was possible that we would come _____
_____

40. it was possible that he would bring _____
_____

ver to see

Present Indicative: veo, ves, ve, vemos, veis, ven   I see, etc.

Imperfect: veía, veías, veía, veíamos, veíais, veían   I was seeing, etc.

Preterit: vi, viste, vio, vimos, visteis, vieron   I saw, etc.

Future: veré, etc.   I will see, etc.

Conditional: vería, etc.   I would see, etc.

Present Participle: viendo   seeing

Past Participle: visto   seen

Present Subjunctive: vea, veas, vea, veamos, veáis, vean   that I see/will see, etc.

Imperfect Subjunctive: viera (viese), etc.   that I saw/would see, etc.; if I saw, etc.

Present Perfect Subjunctive: haya visto, etc.   that I saw/have seen, etc.

Pluperfect Subjunctive: hubiera (hubiese) visto   that I had seen/would have seen, etc.; if I had seen, etc.

19 Irregular Past Participles

Besides the irregular verbs whose past participles have been listed previously, several verbs, otherwise regular, have irregular past participles. Common ones are:

abrir	*abierto*	*morir*	*muerto*
cubrir	*cubierto*	*resolver*	*resuelto*
escribir	*escrito*	*volver*	*vuelto*

Others:
descubrir (*descubierto*) to discover   *revolver* (*revuelto*) to stir
describir (*descrito*) to describe   *devolver* (*devuelto*) to give back, return

Aplicación

Write in English:

1. que yo vea _____

2. si ellos hubieran descubierto _____

_____

3. si viéramos _____

4. que hayas visto _____

5. verías _____

6. vimos _____

7. hemos descrito _____

8. que él vea _____

9. él habrá muerto _____

10. Uds. veían _____

11. verás _____

12. yo había resuelto _____

13. vemos _____

14. viste _____

15. ellos habrían vuelto _____

Mastery Test

Write in Spanish:

1. we do not see _____

2. they were seeing _____

3. if you (pl., fam.) saw _____

_____

4. he had not written _____

5. I hope you (s., fam.) see _____

_____

6. she did not see _____

7. have they discovered? _____

_____

8. it's possible that I saw _____

9. we would see _____

10. he has not covered _____

11. I was seeing _____

12. she will not see _____

13. it's possible that he has seen _____

14. they would have opened _____

15. don't you (pl., fam.) see? _____

_____

Repaso de verbos irregulares

A. Write in English:

1. él habrá venido _____

2. Uds. tuvieron _____

3. ellos irían _____

4. Ud. dirá _____

5. fuiste _____

6. él querría _____

7. vemos _____

8. fui _____

9. traje _____

10. él salía _____

11. habrás sabido _____

12. ellos estuvieran _____

13. habíamos podido _____

14. yo habría puesto _____

15. que ellas den _____

16. que yo ande _____

17. si ellas cayeran _____

18. que valgamos _____

19. él había cabido _____

20. oíste _____

21. él habrá satisfecho _____

22. él no haría _____

23. conducimos _____

24. Uds. asirían _____

25. traducías _____

26. que haya habido _____

27. ella dice _____

28. vamos _____

29. habíamos sido _____

30. Uds. tendrán _____

31. ellos venían _____

32. que ellas hayan visto _____

33. Uds. quisieron _____

34. él traía _____

35. ellos dieron _____

36. que estés _____

37. Ud. salía _____

38. poníais _____

39. podemos _____

40. sabremos _____

41. habíamos oído _____

42. habrás valido _____

43. que yo haya hecho _____

44. satisfarás _____

45. caeré _____

46. ella anduvo _____

47. que él quepa _____

48. habrá _____

49. ellos tradujeron _____

50. que yo conduzca _____

B. Write in Spanish:

1. I hope she is (*ser*) _____

2. we will have come _____

3. you (s., fam.) were saying _____

_____

4. does he go? _____

5. it was impossible for us to see _____

6. they might have _____

7. you (s., fam.) had wanted _____

_____

8. I should bring _____

9. it's possible that I will know _____

10. we are (*estar*) _____

11. you (s., fam.) will have put _____

_____

12. I was able (imperf) _____

13. we have not given _____

14. he did not go out _____

15. I hope you (pl., fam.) didn't fall _____

_____

16. we were hearing _____

17. he fell _____

18. we would be worth _____

19. he walked _____

20. I fitted _____

21. I will not do _____

22. they used to translate _____

_____

23. they would have seized _____

_____

24. he led _____

25. it's possible that you (s., fam.) will deduce _____ _____

26. there would be _____

27. he will have said _____

28. I would go _____

29. it's possible that they have seen _____ _____

30. I hope they have _____

31. he was coming _____

32. she was wanting _____

33. you (pl., fam.) have been (*ser*) _____

34. let's not bring _____

35. he doesn't know _____

36. you (s., fam.) could (pret) _____ _____

37. we will be (*estar*) _____

38. give! (pl.) _____

39. I would go out _____

40. you (pl., fam.) will put _____

41. it's possible that I will hear _____ _____

42. we will not walk _____

43. I will fit _____

44. you (s., for.) have been worth _____ _____

45. if we satisfied _____

46. we did not do _____

47. I am falling _____

48. it's possible that we will seize _____ _____

49. they might have been (*ser*) _____

50. if he led _____

Repaso general 2

A. Write in English:

1. pensamos _____

2. Ud. abrió _____

3. que pierdan _____

4. ella contesta _____

5. entiendo _____

6. llegué _____

7. Ud. dirá _____

8. él se divirtió _____

9. yo duermo _____

10. trajimos _____

11. hice _____

12. ellos vendrán _____

13. que sepas _____

14. si yo pusiera _____

15. que podamos _____

16. Ud. escoja _____

17. si volviéramos _____

18. que ellos saquen _____

19. que ellos distinguen _____

20. si yo buscara _____

21. leeré _____

22. Uds. conocerían _____

23. ellos tendrán _____

24. di _____

25. verás _____

26. él insinúa _____

27. que yo empiece _____

28. enviamos _____

29. que yo haya jugado _____

30. que yo confíe _____

B.   Write in Spanish:

1. We were writing _____

2. he understands _____

3. they live _____

4. they were traveling _____

5. you (s., fam.) keep _____

6. you (pl., for.) were bringing _____

7. do we say? _____

8. he wants _____

9. he dressed himself _____

10. they did not see _____

11. we went out _____

12. if he put _____

13. they have not done _____

14. I don't know (*saber*) _____

15. you (s., fam.) could (pret.) _____

_____

16. we directed _____

17. I looked for _____

18. if they chose _____

19. explain! (pl., for.) _____

20. I hope he arrives _____

21. you (s., fam.) are worth _____

22. did they read? _____

23. if you (s., fam.) gave _____

_____

24. let's not go _____

25. I hope he has _____

26. it's possible that they will play _____

27. I denied _____

28. I hope he continues _____

29. I did not begin _____

30. it's impossible that they will send _____

Repaso general 3

A. Write in English:

1. empecé _____

2. que yo juegue _____

3. negábamos _____

4. ella continúa _____

5. ellos enviarán _____

6. Ud. consigue _____

7. tuve _____

8. condujiste _____

9. yo salía _____

10. supieron _____

11. él oiría _____

12. Ud. cabe _____

13. él ponga _____

14. podríamos _____

15. vengo _____

16. ellos habrán muerto _____

17. yo reía _____

18. él contribuía _____

19. él destruye _____

20. Ud. poseía _____

21. que construyan _____

22. él pierde _____

23. servíamos _____

24. él conocía _____

25. ella hirió _____

26. yo piense _____

27. echaron _____

28. él habrá perdido _____

29. escuchabas _____

30. ella había vuelto _____

B. Write in Spanish:

1. you (pl, fam.) were playing _____

_____

2. if they began _____

3. I continue _____

4. it's possible that I will trust _____

_____

5. they do not read _____

6. he did not want _____

7. they would be (ser) _____

8. I am not correcting _____

9. I went _____

10. he said _____

11. it's possible that I will see _____

_____

12. you (s., for.) were falling _____

_____

13. I did _____

14. I have put _____

15. they will go out _____

16. it's possible that I will read _____

_____

17. we had slept _____

18. if we laughed _____

19. it's possible that he will die _____

_____

20. they did not believe _____

21. I sent _____

22. do you (pl., fam.) consent? _____

_____

23. I hope they don't destroy _____

_____

24. he was repeating _____

25. we used to lose _____

26. you (s., fam.) do not return _____

_____

27. we were spending _____

28. I was living _____

29. you (pl., fam.) understood _____

_____

30. they have opened _____

20 Final Review

Featuring a mixture of reflexive, stem-changing, and irregular verbs, as well as verbs with orthographic changes, the verbs in this final review will reinforce your command of the kinds of conjugations you have learned throughout the book.

Moler   to grind

Present Indicative: *muelo, mueles, muele,* molemos, moléis, *muelen*   I grind, etc.

Imperfect: molía, etc.   I was grinding, etc.

Preterit: molí, etc.   I ground, etc.

Future: moleré, etc.   I will grind, etc.

Conditional: molería, etc.   I would grind, etc.

Present Participle: moliendo   grinding

Past Participle: molido   ground

Present Subjunctive: *muela, muelas, muela,* molamos, moláis, *muelan*   that I grind/will grind, etc.

Imperfect Subjunctive: moliera (moliese), etc.   that I ground/would grind, etc.; if I ground, etc.

Present Perfect Subjunctive: haya molido, etc.   that I ground/have ground, etc.

Pluperfect Subjunctive: hubiera (hubiese) molido, etc.   that I had ground/would have ground, etc.; if I had ground, etc.

Fregar   to scrub

Present Indicative: *friego, friegas, friega,* fregamos, fregáis, *friegan*   I scrub, etc.

Imperfect: fregaba, etc.   I was scrubbing, etc.

Preterit: fregué, etc.   I scrubbed, etc.

Future: fregaré, etc.   I will scrub, etc.

Conditional: fregaría, etc.   I would scrub, etc.

Present Participle: fregando   scrubbing

Past Participle: fregado   scrubbed

Present Subjunctive: *friegue, friegues, friegue,* freguemos, freguéis, *frieguen*   that I scrub/will scrub, etc.

Imperfect Subjunctive: fregara (fregase), etc.   that I scrubbed/would scrub, etc.; if I scrubbed, etc.

Present Perfect Subjunctive: haya fregado, etc.   that I scrub/have scrubbed, etc.

Pluperfect Subjunctive: hubiera (hubiese) fregado, etc.   that I had scrubbed/would have scrubbed, etc.; if I had scrubbed, etc.

Descender   to descend

Present Indicative: *desciendo, desciendes, desciende,* descendemos, descendéis, *descienden*   I descend, etc.

Imperfect: descendía, etc.   I was descending, etc.

Preterit: descendí, etc.   I descended, etc.

Future: descenderé, etc.   I will descend, etc.

Conditional: descendería, etc.   I would descend, etc.

Present Participle: descendiendo   descending

Past Participle: descendido   descended

Present Subjunctive: *descienda, desciendas, descienda,* descendamos, descendáis, *desciendan*   that I descend/will descend, etc.

Imperfect Subjunctive: descendiera (descendiese), etc.   that I descended/would descend, etc.; if I descended, etc.

Present Perfect Subjunctive: haya descendido, etc.   that I descended/have descended, etc.

Pluperfect Subjunctive: hubiera (hubiese) descendido, etc.   that I had descended/would have descended, etc.; if I had descended, etc.

Yacer   to lie, to rest

Present Indicative: *yazgo,* yaces, yace, yacemos, yacéis, yacen   I lie, etc.

Imperfect: yacía, etc.   I was lying, etc.

Preterit: yací, etc.   I lay, etc.

Future: yaceré, etc.   I will lie, etc.

Conditional: yacería, etc.   I would lie, etc.

Present Participle: yaciendo   lying

Past Participle: yacido   lain

Present Subjunctive: *yazga, yazgas, yazga, yazgamos, yazgáis, yazgan*   that I lie/will lie, etc.

Imperfect Subjunctive: yaciera (yaciese), etc.   that I lay/would lie, etc.; if I lay, etc.

Present Perfect Subjunctive: haya yacido, etc.   that I lay/have lain, etc.

Pluperfect Subjunctive: hubiera (hubiese) yacido, etc.   that I had lain/would have lain, etc.; if I had lain, etc.

Torcer   to twist

Present Indicative: *tuerzo, tuerces, tuerce,* torcemos, torcéis, *tuercen*   I twist, etc.

Imperfect: torcía, etc.   I was twisting, etc.

Preterit: torcí, etc.   I twisted, etc.

Future: torceré, etc.   I will twist, etc.

Conditional: torcería, etc.   I would twist, etc.

Present Participle: torciendo   twisting

Past Participle: torcido   twisted

Present Subjunctive: *tuerza, tuerzas, tuerza,* torzamos, torzáis, *tuerzan*   that I twist/will twist, etc.

Imperfect Subjunctive: torciera (torciese), etc.   that I twisted/would twist, etc.; if I twisted, etc.

Present Perfect Subjunctive: haya torcido, etc.   that I twisted/have twisted, etc.

Pluperfect Subjunctive: hubiera (hubiese) torcido, etc.   that I had twisted/would have twisted, etc.; if I had twisted, etc.

Surgir   to spring up, to arise

Present Indicative: *surjo,* surges, surge, surgimos, surgís, surgen   I spring up, etc.

Imperfect: surgía, etc.   I was springing up, etc.

Preterit: surgí, etc.   I sprang up, etc.

Future: surgiré, etc.   I will spring up, etc.

Conditional: surgiría, etc.   I would spring up, etc.

Present Participle: surgiendo   springing up

Past Participle: surgido   sprang up

Present Subjunctive: *surja, surjas, surja, surjamos, surjáis, surjan*   that I spring up/will spring up, etc.

Imperfect Subjunctive: surgiera (surgiese), etc.   that I sprang up/would spring up, etc.; if I sprang up, etc.

Present Perfect Subjunctive: haya surgido, etc.   that I sprang up/have sprung up, etc.

Pluperfect Subjunctive: hubiera (hubiese) surgido, etc.   that I had sprung up/would have sprung up, etc.; if I had sprung up, etc.

Mecer   to swing, to rock

Present Indicative: *mezo,* meces, mece, mecemos, mecéis, mecen   I swing, etc.

Imperfect: mecía, etc.   I was swinging, etc.

Preterit: mecí, etc.   I swung, etc.

Future: meceré, etc.   I will swing, etc.

Conditional: mecería, etc.   I would swing, etc.

Present Participle: meciendo   swinging

Past Participle: mecido   swung

Present Subjunctive: *meza, mezas, meza, mezamos, mezáis, mezan*   that I swing/will swing, etc.

Imperfect Subjunctive: meciera (meciese), etc.   that I swung/would swing, etc.; if I swung, etc.

Present Perfect Subjunctive: haya mecido, etc.   that I swung/have swung, etc.

Pluperfect Subjunctive: hubiera (hubiese) mecido, etc.   that I had swung/would have swung, etc.; if I had swung, etc.

Reñir   to quarrel, to fight

Present Indicative: *riño, riñes, riñe,* reñimos, reñís, *riñen*   I quarrel, etc.

Imperfect: reñía, etc.   I was quarrelling, etc.

Preterit: reñí, etc.   I quarrelled, etc.

Future: reñiré, etc.   I will quarrel, etc.

Conditional: reñiría, etc.   I would quarrel, etc.

Present Participle: *riñendo*   quarrelling

Past Participle: reñido   quarrelled

Present Subjunctive: *riña, riñas, riña, riñamos, riñáis, riñan*   that I quarrel/will quarrel, etc.

Imperfect Subjunctive: *riñera (riñese), etc.*   that I quarrelled/would quarrel, etc.; if I quarrelled, etc.

Present Perfect Subjunctive: haya reñido, etc.   that I quarrelled/have quarrelled, etc.

Pluperfect Subjunctive: hubiera (hubiese) reñido, etc.   that I had quarrelled/would have quarrelled, etc.; if I had quarrelled, etc.

Avergonzar   to embarrass

Present Indicative: *avergüenzo, avergüenzas, avergüenza,* avergonzamos, avergonzáis, *avergüenzan*   I embarrass, etc.

Imperfect: avergonzaba, etc.   I was embarrassing, etc.

Preterit: avergoncé, etc.   I embarrassed, etc.

Future: avergonzaré, etc.   I will embarrass, etc.

Conditional: avergonzaría, etc.   I would embarrass, etc.

Present Participle: avergonzando   embarrassing

Past Participle: avergonzado   embarrassed

Present Subjunctive: *avergüence, avergüences, avergüence,* avergoncemos, avergoncéis, *avergüencen*   that I embarrass/will embarrass, etc.

Imperfect Subjunctive: avergonzara (avergonzase), etc.   that I embarrassed/would embarrass, etc.; if I embarrassed, etc.

Present Perfect Subjunctive: haya avergonzado, etc.   that I embarrassed/have embarrassed, etc.

Pluperfect Subjunctive: hubiera (hubiese) avergonzado, etc.   that I had embarrassed/would have embarrassed, etc.; if I had embarrassed, etc.

Influir   to influence

Present Indicative: *influyo, influyes, influye,* influimos, influís, *influyen*   I influence, etc.

Imperfect: influía, etc.   I was influencing, etc.

Preterit: influí, etc.   I influenced, etc.

Future: influiré, etc.   I will influence, etc.

Conditional: influiría, etc.   I would influence, etc.

Present Participle: *influyendo*   influencing

Past Participle: influido   influenced

Present Subjunctive: *influya, influyas, influya, influyamos, influyáis, influyan*   that I influence/will influence, etc.

Imperfect Subjunctive: *influyera (influyese), etc.*   that I influenced/would influenced, etc.; if I influenced, etc.

Present Perfect Subjunctive: haya influido, etc.   that I influenced/have influenced, etc.

Pluperfect Subjunctive: hubiera (hubiese) influido, etc.   that I had influenced/would have influenced, etc.; if I had influenced, etc.

Roer   to gnaw

Present Indicative: roo, roes, roe, roemos, roéis, roen   I gnaw, etc.

Imperfect: roía, etc.   I was gnawing, etc.

Preterit: roí, etc.   I gnawed, etc.

Future: roeré, etc.   I will gnaw, etc.

Conditional: roería, etc.   I would gnaw, etc.

Present Participle: *royendo*   gnawing

Past Participle: roído   gnawed

Present Subjunctive: roa, roas, roa, roamos, roáis, roan   that I gnaw/will gnaw, etc.

Imperfect Subjunctive: *royera (royese)*, etc.   that I gnawed/would gnaw, etc.; if I gnawed, etc.

Present Perfect Subjunctive: haya roído, etc.   that I gnawed/have gnawed, etc.

Pluperfect Subjunctive: hubiera (hubiese) roído, etc.   that I had gnawed/would have gnawed, etc.; if I had gnawed, etc.

Erguir(se)   to straighten (oneself) up

Present Indicative: (me) *yergo*, (te) *yergues*, (se) *yergue*, (nos) erguimos, (os) erguís, (se) *yerguen*   I straighten (myself) up, etc

Imperfect: erguía, etc.   I was straightening up, etc.

Preterit: erguí, etc.   I straightened up, etc.

Future: erguiré, etc.   I will straighten up, etc.

Conditional: erguiría, etc.   I would straighten up, etc.

Present Participle: *irguiendo*   straightening up

Past Participle: erguido   straightened up

Present Subjunctive: *yerga, yergas, yerga, yergamos, irgáis, yergan*   that I straighten up/will straighten up, etc.

Imperfect Subjunctive: *irguiera (irguiese)*, etc.   that I straightened up/would straighten up, etc.; if I straightened up, etc.

Present Perfect Subjunctive: haya erguido, etc.   that I straightened up/have straightened up, etc.

Pluperfect Subjunctive: hubiera (hubiese) erguido, etc.   that I had straightened up/would have straightened up, etc.; if I had straightened up, etc.

Discernir   to discern

Present Indicative: *discierno, disciernes, discierne*, discernimos, discernís, *disciernen*   I discern, etc.

Imperfect: discernía, etc.   I was discerning, etc.

Preterit: discerní, etc.   I discerned, etc.

Future: discerniré, etc.   I will discern, etc.

Conditional: discerniría, etc.   I would discern, etc.

Present Participle: discerniendo   discerning

Past Participle: discernido   discerned

Present Subjunctive: *discierna, disciernas, discierna,* discernamos, discernáis, disciernan   that I discern/ will discern, etc.

Imperfect Subjunctive: discerniera (discerniese), etc.   that I discerned/would discern, etc.; if I discerned, etc.

Present Perfect Subjunctive: haya discernido, etc.   that I discerned/have discerned, etc.

Pluperfect Subjunctive: hubiera (hubiese) discernido, etc.   that I had discerned/would have discerned, etc.; if I had discerned, etc.

Zurcir   to mend, to darn

Present Indicative: *zurzo,* zurces, zurce, zurcimos, zurcís, zurcen   I mend, etc.

Imperfect: zurcía, etc.   I was mending, etc.

Preterit: zurcí, etc.   I mended, etc.

Future: zurciré, etc.   I will mend, etc.

Conditional: zurciría, etc.   I would mend, etc.

Present Participle: zurciendo   mending

Past Participle: zurcido   mended

Present Subjunctive: *zurza, zurzas, zurza, zurzamos, zurzáis, zurzan*   that I mend/will mend, etc.

Imperfect Subjunctive: zurciera (zurciese), etc.   that I mended/would mend, etc.; if I mended, etc.

Present Perfect Subjunctive: haya zurcido, etc.   that I mended/have mended, etc.

Pluperfect Subjunctive: hubiera (hubiese) zurcido, etc.   that I had mended/would have mended, etc.; if I had mended, etc.

Entrenar(se)   to train (oneself)

Present Indicative: (me) entreno, (te) entrenas, (se) entrena, (nos) entrenamos, (os) entrenáis, (se) entrenan   I train, etc.

Imperfect: entrenaba, etc.   I was training, etc.

Preterit: entrené, etc.   I trained, etc.

Future: entrenaré, etc.   I will train, etc.

Conditional: entrenaría, etc.   I would train, etc.

Present Participle: entrenando   training

Past Participle: entrenado   trained

Present Subjunctive: (me) entrene, (te) entrenes, (se) entrene, (nos) entrenemos, (os) entrenéis, (se) entrenen   that I train/will train, etc.

Imperfect Subjunctive: entrenara (entrenase), etc.   that I trained/would train, etc.; if I trained, etc.

Present Perfect Subjunctive: haya entrenado, etc.   that I trained/have trained, etc.

Pluperfect Subjunctive: hubiera (hubiese) entrenado, etc.   that I had trained/would have trained, etc.; if I had trained, etc.

Enojar(se)   to get angry (oneself)

Present Indicative: (me) enojo, (te) enojas, (se) enoja, (nos) enojamos, (os) enojáis, (se) enojan   I get angry, etc.

Imperfect: enojaba, etc.   I was getting angry, etc.

Preterit: enojé, etc.   I got angry, etc.

Future: enojaré, etc.   I will get angry, etc.

Conditional: enojaría, etc.   I would get angry, etc.

Present Participle: enojando   getting angry

Past Participle: enojado   gotten angry

Present Subjunctive: (me) enoje, (te) enojes, (se) enoje, (nos) enojemos, (os) enojéis, (se) enojen
            that I get angry/will get angry, etc.

Imperfect Subjunctive: enojara (enojase), etc.   that I got angry/would get angry, etc.; if I got angry, etc.

Present Perfect Subjunctive: haya enojado, etc.   that I got angry/have gotten angry, etc.

Pluperfect Subjunctive: hubiera (hubiese) enojado, etc.   that I had gotten angry/would have gotten angry,
            etc.; if I had gotten angry, etc.

Para practicar 1

Write the verbs in the present, imperfect, and preterit tenses in the person indicated:

1. yo (aprender) _____

2. Ud. (zurcir) _____

3. ella (pecar) _____

4. nosotros (avergonzar) _____

5. vosotros (erguirse) _____

6. tú (sollozar) _____

7. ellas (vestirse) _____

8. ellos (caber) _____

9. Ud. (oler) _____

10. yo (yacer) _____

11. él (exponer) _____

12. Uds. (apaciguar) _____

13. tú (graduarse) _____

14. yo (roer) _____

15. ella (enojarse) _____

16. nosotros (poseer) _____

17. tú (almorzar) _____

18. ellos (revolver) _____

19. Ud. (huir) _____

20. yo (salir) _____

21. ellas (desnegar) _____

22. vosotros (suponer) _____

23. él (levantarse) _____

24. nosotros (compadecer) _____

25. tú (ahogar) _____

Para practicar 2

A. Change to the plural of the same tense:

1. voy _____

2. has estado _____

3. él arriesgaría _____

4. ella había querido _____

5. se divirtió _____

6. te levantaste _____

7. hubiera escuchado _____

8. estoy traduciendo _____

9. yo haya fregado _____

10. dormirías _____

B. Change to the singular person of the corresponding compound tense:

1. avergonzáramos _____

2. tomabais _____

3. hablaríamos _____

4. dormirán _____

5. no desconfíen _____

6. estamos comiendo _____

7. dijimos _____

8. sintiesen _____

9. oleremos _____

10. vistieseis _____

Para practicar 3

A. Write the present perfect in the person indicated:

1. yo (estudiar) _____

2. María (necesitar) _____

3. nosotros (contar) _____

4. vosotros (ofender) _____

5. ustedes (decir) _____

6. tú (ser) _____

7. yo (moler) _____

8. Ernesto (suponer) _____

9. Luis y María (dormir) _____

10. vosotros (describir) _____

B. Write the conditional in the person indicated:

1. Juan complace _____

2. vosotros ofenderéis _____

3. tú has dicho _____

4. ellas sostendrán _____

5. Ud. se habrá entrenado _____

6. nosotros nos hubiésemos mecido _____

_____

7. yo extinga _____

8. María y Ana habían sabido _____

9. Uds. venderán _____

10. ¿acertará él? _____

Para practicar 4

A. Write the present participles of the following verbs:

1. escuchar _____
2. carecer _____
3. medir _____
4. estar _____
5. ser _____

6. perseguir _____
7. advertir _____
8. vestirse _____
9. servir _____
10. huir _____

B. Write the past participles of the following verbs:

1. abrir _____
2. ejercer _____
3. suponer _____
4. revolver _____
5. hacer _____

6. descubrir _____
7. agradecer _____
8. satisfacer _____
9. costar _____
10. volver _____

Para practicar 5

A. Write the verbs in the present indicative in the person indicated:

Ud.

servir	influir	vivir	decaer	oler
_____	_____	_____	_____	_____

B. Write the verbs in the preterit in the person indicated:

yo

reñir	sonreír	seguir	contraer	resolver
_____	_____	_____	_____	_____

C. Write the verbs in the present subjunctive in the person indicated:

vosotros

comprender	convenir	encontrar	insinuar	repetir
_____	_____	_____	_____	_____

D. Write the verbs in the future perfect in the person indicated:

ella

morir	perder	escribir	proponer	caber
_____	_____	_____	_____	_____

E. Write the verbs in the imperfect indicative in the person indicated:

nosotros

oír	enriquecerse	desconocer	negar	unir
_____	_____	_____	_____	_____

Para practicar 6

Write the verbs in the present subjunctive in the person indicated:

tú

rascar	asir	fregar	torcer	cargar
_____	_____	_____	_____	_____

nosotros

escuchar	conducir	descontinuar	destruir	negar
_____	_____	_____	_____	_____

él

contraer	creer	delinquir	valer	contestar
_____	_____	_____	_____	_____

vosotros

secar	gemir	habituarse	aborrecer	esconder
_____	_____	_____	_____	_____

yo

dormir	surgir	impedir	preparar	decir
_____	_____	_____	_____	_____

146

Aplicación 1

Write in English:

1. que yo tenga _____

2. que Juan y Pedro se diviertan _____

3. habías salido _____

4. ellas estaban consintiendo _____

_____

5. habré escrito _____

6. él hablaría _____

7. Uds. habían revuelto _____

8. ellos midieron _____

9. yo advertía _____

10. que Ud. sintiera _____

11. si hubieseis movido _____

12. ¿cuándo empezarás? _____

13. ¡ven! _____

14. si te hubieras divertido _____

15. ella habría creído _____

16. ¡no confiéis! _____

17. ¿vas a jugar? _____

18. secaremos _____

19. yo estaba limpiando _____

20. ella necesitó _____

21. podríamos _____

22. ofendiste _____

23. Ud. encuentre _____

24. Juan reía _____

25. que tuvisteis _____

26. nos vestíamos _____

27. habremos sollozado _____

28. él tuvo _____

29. estábamos estudiando _____

30. no habíamos encontrado _____

31. si durmiéramos _____

32. que hayas viajado _____

33. Uds. conocerían _____

34. ellos necesitan _____

35. que yo midiera _____

Aplicación 2

Change each verb to express past time in the same person and mood:

1. dormimos _____
2. influyas _____
3. él abre _____
4. he revuelto _____
5. habéis elegido _____
6. Uds. ruegan _____
7. desconocéis _____
8. no beban _____
9. somos _____
10. pasaremos _____
11. encontramos _____
12. exponga _____
13. se enriquezcan _____

14. creemos _____
15. habéis aceptado _____
16. carguen _____
17. son _____
18. distinguís _____
19. hemos convocado _____
20. compitas _____
21. están corrigiendo _____
22. obedezcamos _____
23. finjáis _____
24. están _____
25. aborrezceremos _____

Aplicación 3

Change from singular to plural in the same tense:

1. estoy oliendo _____
2. viví _____
3. yo admiraba _____
4. él merecía _____
5. hayas desaparecido _____
6. Ud. habría ejercido _____
7. obligues _____

8. gemirás _____
9. ella compusiera _____
10. yo aprendería _____
11. ella riñó _____
12. él haya conseguido _____
13. ¡corra! _____
14. yo habría pensado _____

15. huyas _____

16. me estoy habituando a _____

_____

17. ha _____

18. has colgado _____

19. hubieras desconfiado _____

20. no esparzas _____

21. pecaré _____

22. sonreíste _____

23. Ud. haya dormido _____

24. me sentaría _____

25. habías erguido _____

Aplicación 4

Change each simple tense to a corresponding compound tense, keeping the person of the original verb:

1. hable _____

2. comieron _____

3. estuvisteis _____

4. pasarán _____

5. no confiarais _____

6. extingas _____

7. moveremos _____

8. muelan _____

9. sintáis _____

10. persigamos _____

11. entrarás _____

12. carecieses _____

13. te enriquecerás _____

14. ofrecen _____

15. decaerías _____

16. será _____

17. colocaríais _____

18. huyó _____

19. influyo _____

20. acordaran _____

21. aprobaste _____

22. asistirías _____

23. llegaréis _____

24. delinquieseis _____

25. rió _____

Aplicación 5

Change from present to imperfect subjunctive:

1. necesitemos _____

2. ruegue _____

3. pagues _____

4. preparéis _____

5. ponga _____

6. produzca _____

7. Pedro y Elena abran _____

_____

8. apacigüe _____

9. impidan _____

10. mezan _____

11. compadezcáis _____

12. prosigas _____

13. paguen _____

14. complazca _____

15. juguemos _____

16. tenga _____

17. coloque _____

18. apagues _____

19. emprendamos _____

20. tome _____

21. repitáis _____

22. arriesguen _____

23. enseñe _____

24. satisfaga _____

25. encoja _____

Mastery Test 1

Translate into Spanish:

1. I will decide _____

2. we are demanding _____

3. if they had seized _____

4. Juan and Pedro ate _____

5. you (pl., fam.) would spend _____

6. I have lied _____

7. she listens _____

8. we were coming _____

9. that you (pl., for.) would read _____

10. he has remembered _____

11. I shall not fall _____

12. we had _____

13. if I had paid _____

14. I hope we reach _____

15. I return _____

16. he has _____

17. he would not have prayed _____

18. it's possible that she has seen _____

19. we were quarreling _____

20. you (s., fam.) used to sleep _____

21. he walked _____

22. did she scatter? _____

23. you (pl., fam.) replied _____

24. were you (s., for.) serving? _____

25. will she run? _____

26. we smile _____

27. it's possible that Gil, Ana, and Luis will seize _____

28. they used to carry _____

29. I do not believe it _____

30. I will have ground _____

31. I hope they don't convince _____

32. it is raining _____

33. they sold _____

34. you (sin., for.) returned _____

35. they would have dressed _____

Mastery Test 2

Translate into English:

1. comeré _____

2. si hubierais jugado _____

3. yazgo _____

4. competíamos _____

5. él vencería _____

6. Ud. cabe _____

7. ella había convencido _____

8. ellas tropezaron _____

9. Uds. estaban preparando _____

10. que ellos nieguen _____

11. admiro _____

12. he comido _____

13. ellas hablarán _____

14. ¡no decidas! _____

15. si Uds. hubiesen hablado _____

16. que yo mantenga _____

17. hemos dicho _____

18. Ud. habría encontrado _____

19. me lavaba _____

20. estabais pensando _____

21. ellos no cargaban _____

22. habías avergonzado _____

23. desafiaremos _____

24. habré encendido _____

25. exigís _____

26. ella había supuesto _____

27. Uds. están mintiendo _____

28. María y José pagarán _____
_____

29. ejercisteis _____

30. se vistieron _____

31. estábamos mordiendo _____

32. yo continuaría _____

33. si Ud. indicara _____

34. sabías _____

35. ¡no pares! _____

Mastery Test 3

Translate into Spanish using reflexive verbs:

1. it's possible that he washed _____

2. I dressed _____

3. we have amused ourselves _____

4. she combed her hair _____

5. they used to wash _____

6. you (pl., for.) have gotten up _____

7. if they had remembered _____

8. he was washing _____

9. I shall grow accustomed to _____

10. you (pl., fam.) washed _____

11. if she had gotten angry _____

12. let's dress! _____

13. I am going to bed _____

14. I hope they wash up _____

15. you (s., fam.) would have remembered _____

16. she is training _____

17. he had gone to bed _____

18. they will have tried hard _____

19. we may sit _____

20. she is becoming rich _____

21. Miguel has gotten up _____

22. I might straighten up _____

23. they grew accustomed to _____

24. she used to amuse herself _____

25. I shall get up _____

26. do not sit! (pl., fam.) _____

27. they are dressing _____

28. if we graduated _____

29. are we trying hard? _____

30. I hope you (s., for.) have washed up _____

31. they would go to bed _____

32. I amuse myself _____

33. María used to comb her hair _____

34. he would have trained _____

35. we got angry _____

Mastery Test 4

Change each simple tense into a compound one in the same person:

1. tome _____
2. medimos _____
3. desconfiarás _____
4. obedece _____
5. se acostaba _____
6. ejercieron _____
7. distinguiese _____
8. dispongas _____
9. influyáis _____
10. sollozaréis _____
11. acierte _____
12. expusiéramos _____
13. elegirán _____
14. hablaríamos _____
15. me acuesto _____
16. subes _____
17. aborrecerán _____
18. moveríamos _____

19. quepamos _____

20. obedecéis _____

21. oliesen _____

22. eligió _____

23. corrigiéramos _____

24. explicase _____

25. llueve _____

Repaso 1

Write in English:

1. él habrá venido _____

2. olisteis _____

3. que digas _____

4. Elena rió _____

5. somos _____

6. riño _____

7. Ud. cupo _____

8. si delinquiéramos _____

9. que Uds. quieran _____

10. estamos cayendo _____

11. ellos anduvieron _____

12. él huele _____

13. hemos conducido _____

14. habrías dicho _____

15. ella erraba _____

16. dierais _____

17. dedujiste _____

18. que yo haya dicho _____

19. si ellas bendijeran _____

20. yo iría _____

21. habrás hecho _____

22. ellos satisfarán _____

23. que vayamos _____

24. no pondrías _____

25. si Ud. saliese _____

Repaso 2

Change each verb to represent more than one person in the same tense:

1. acabo _____

2. hablas _____

3. comiste _____

4. habría partido _____

5. estudiará _____

6. ella comprenda _____

7. he preguntado _____

8. beberás _____

9. ella escuchaba _____

10. abrí _____

11. entraste _____

12. vivió _____

13. hubiera tomado _____

14. yo tema _____

15. habré estudiado _____

16. ¿se habrá graduado? _____

17. yo estaba llevando _____

18. él escribiría _____

19. comprenderé _____

20. Ud. entre _____

21. él haya leído _____

22. yo había vendido _____

23. has trabajado _____

24. ella prepararía _____

25. me hubiese amado _____

Repaso 3

Write in Spanish:

1. I hope I understand _____

2. if you (s., fam.) had spoken _____

3. that we would say _____

4. it's possible that you (s., fam.) won't smile _____

5. if she had disappeared _____

6. it's possible that I won't discover _____

7. it's impossible that he slept _____

8. if you (pl., fam.) had noticed _____

9. it's possible that we will lie _____

10. if she combed her hair _____

11. it's possible that you (s., for.) mistrusted _____

156

12. I hope they learn _____

13. if you (pl., fam.) stumbled _____

14. that I would go _____

15. it's possible that she will sell _____

16. it's possible that Ana and Juan will compete _____

17. it's possible that he will dress _____

18. if we had needed _____

19. if they had gone to bed _____

20. it's possible that you (pl., for.) have not twisted _____

21. I hope she remembers _____

22. I would warm _____

23. it's possible that we taught _____

24. if he followed _____

25. it's possible that you (pl., fam.) have gotten up _____

Repaso 4

Write in English:

1. ella prepara _____

2. ¿están ellos entrando? _____

3. habremos impedido _____

4. llegué _____

5. habréis satisfecho _____

6. ellos están desconfiando _____

7. habíamos compuesto _____

8. ellos advertirían _____

9. él continuaba _____

10. yo me yergo _____

11. ¡bendícenos! _____

12. habrás analizado _____

13. si detuviéramos _____

14. que él conduzca _____

15. sollozarás _____

16. yo habría reñido _____

17. Elisa y Marta habían pensado _____

_____

18. si consiguiésemos _____

19. estudiaríais _____

20. habremos valido _____

21. que ellos viviesen _____

22. ¡no mintáis! _____

23. ella haya impuesto _____

24. que Uds. hubieran perseguido _____

25. estabas mostrando _____

26. si ellos se acostaran _____

27. ella zurció _____

28. Ud. había abrazado _____

29. ella querría _____

30. nevará _____

31. Uds. hayan descendido _____

32. que vivamos _____

33. que él no coloque _____

34. erais _____

35. que yo haya roído _____

36. Ud. habría hecho _____

37. compongo _____

38. si fuésemos (*to go*) _____

39. si hubiérais partido _____

40. que ellas consiguiesen _____

Repaso 5

Write in Spanish:

1. I will go _____

2. it's raining _____

3. I hope you (s., for.) sleep _____

4. we had thrown _____

5. they were playing _____

6. she has marked _____

7. if Juan and Ana knew _____

_____

8. she will have exercised _____

9. I would conduct _____

10. enter! (s., fam.) _____

11. it's impossible that we will dispose _____

_____

12. she does not deserve _____

13. if you (pl., for.) had found _____

14. let's not go _____

15. I hope they stop _____

16. he does listen _____

17. if we washed _____

18. I would bother _____

19. María will break the law _____

20. she is worth _____

21. we are travelling _____

22. I am combing my hair _____

23. it's possible that you (pl., for.) (will) influence

_____

24. he had conquered _____

25. they would explain _____

Repaso 6

A. Change each verb from singular to plural in the same tense:

1. parto _____

2. comías _____

3. él unía _____

4. ella había salido _____

5. ¡acuéstese! _____

6. ¡no me pidas! _____

7. yo corregiría _____

8. Ud. haya confesado _____

9. ella se habrá acostado _____

10. discernió _____

11. yo me hubiese despertado _____

_____

12. desaparecerás _____

13. bendices _____

14. yo huela _____

15. se peinó _____

B. Write the following verbs in the present subjunctive in the person indicated:

1. tú (marcar) _____

2. ustedes (repetir) _____

3. nosotros (salir) _____

4. yo (caber) _____

5. él (consentir) _____

6. vosotros (explicar) _____

7. Ana y Juan (aborrecer) _____

8. yo (elegir) _____

9. ellos (haber) _____

10. ustedes (hacer) _____

11. ellas (ir) _____

12. nosotros (erguir) _____

13. tú (encoger) _____

14. usted (encontrar) _____

15. ella (complacer) _____

Repaso 7

A. Write the present indicative of the following verbs in the person indicated:

ella

errar	huir	cerrar	gemir	morir	negar
_____	_____	_____	_____	_____	_____

disponer	encontrar	proseguir	haber
_____	_____	_____	_____

B. Write the present subjunctive of the following verbs in the person indicated:

nosotros

contar	revolver	castigar	surgir	lavar(se)	conducir
_____	_____	_____	_____	_____	_____

parecer	sacar	esconder	santiguar
_____	_____	_____	_____

C. Write the imperfect subjunctive of the following verbs in the person indicated:

yo

colegir	mantener	cubrir	perseguir	decaer	andar
_____	_____	_____	_____	_____	_____

acoger	querer	dormir	influir
_____	_____	_____	_____

Repaso 8

Change each simple tense into the corresponding compound tense in the same person:

1. acertaba _____

2. hablen _____

3. hablarían _____

4. dijimos _____

5. mantenemos _____

6. hacíais _____

7. corrían _____

8. advirtieras _____

9. descubriré _____

10. colocaban _____

11. almuercen _____

12. se dispusiese _____

13. adornáis _____

14. me vestiré _____

15. royéramos _____

16. abrías _____

17. ofrezco _____

18. hirieran _____

19. fatigüéis _____

20. supo _____

Answer Key

1 PRESENT

Para practicar

pp. 2–5

(1) acabo	(2) tomo	(1) vendo	(2) bebo	(1) vivo	(2) recibo
acabas	tomas	vendes	bebes	vives	recibes
acaba	toma	vende	bebe	vive	recibe
acaba	toma	vende	bebe	vive	recibe
acabamos	tomamos	vendemos	bebemos	vivimos	recibimos
acabáis	tomáis	vendéis	bebéis	vivís	recibís
acaban	toman	venden	beben	viven	reciben
acaban	toman	venden	beben	viven	reciben

estudio, comprendo, temo, necesito, parto, enseño, vendo.

hablas, asistes, abres, bebes, preguntas, tomas, escuchas.

contesta, abre, aprende, entra, lee, vive, come.

escribe, estudia, acaba, teme, parte, comprende, vende.

aprendemos, asistimos, tomamos, escuchamos, hablamos, vivimos, tememos.

habláis, asistís, bebéis, leéis, tomáis, lleváis, enseñáis.

comen, escriben, necesitan, entran, acaban, leen, viven.

temen, llevan, estudian, preguntan, contestan, comprenden, parten.

Aplicación

pp. 5–6

A.
1. tomamos
2. aprende
3. venden
4. asisto
5. contestas
6. bebe
7. abrimos
8. necesita
9. tomáis
10. lee
11. aprendo
12. tememos
13. recibís
14. escriben
15. abre
16. enseñamos
17. contesto
18. estudiamos
19. abro
20. toma
21. pregunta
22. leen
23. reciben
24. temes
25. leemos

Aplicación (*cont.*)

B.
1. escribimos,
   we write
2. ellos contestan,
   they answer
3. vivimos,
   we live
4. Uds. necesitan,
   you need
5. ellos beben,
   they drink
6. aprendéis,
   you learn
7. ellos venden,
   they sell
8. asistimos,
   we attend
9. Uds. enseñan,
   you teach
10. abrís,
    you open
11. Uds. comprenden,
    you understand
12. ellas escuchan,
    they listen
13. teméis,
    you fear
14. ellas preguntan,
    they ask
15. Uds. leen,
    you read
16. tomamos,
    we take
17. recibimos,
    we receive
18. ellos estudian,
    they study
19. necesitamos,
    we need
20. escribís,
    you write

Mastery Test

pp. 6–7

1. contestamos
2. vendéis
3. él pregunta
4. si ellos venden
5. no necesitamos
6. si estudiamos
7. aprendo
8. ¿escuchan ellos?
9. él no lee
10. Ud. no entra
11. si trabajamos
12. ¿escribes?
13. si ellos preguntan
14. si Uds. toman
15. vendo
16. ella no trabaja
17. ellos no creen
18. ellos esconden
19. si él escribe
20. ¿temes?
21. vivimos
22. él enseña
23. ella teme
24. recibís
25. él abre
26. si ellos no toman
27. si asistimos
28. ¿vende él?
29. estudio
30. creo
31. ellos unen
32. ellos no abren
33. si enseñas
34. él asiste
35. preguntamos
36. ¿aprenden Uds?
37. si ella bebe
38. ¿estudias?
39. Ud. vive
40. ellos entran

2 IMPERFECT

Para practicar

pp. 8–10

tomaba, metía, vivía, compraba, sentía, viajaba, corría.

aprendías, subías, pasabas, guardabas, cosías, esperabas, acababas.

tocaba, amaba, sabía, jugaba, viajaba, comprendía, escribía.

echaba, preparaba, leía, vivía, abría, corría, trabajaba.

estudiábamos, vendíamos, subíamos, comprendíamos, abríamos, preparábamos, tomábamos.

escribíais, trabajabais, comíais, bebíais, recibíais, comprabais, llevabais.

pasaban, caminaban, respondían, subían, hablaban, abrían, sacaban.

acababan, salían, contestaban, vivían, guardaban, corrían, viajaban.

Aplicación

pp. 10–11

A.
1. hablaba
2. vivíamos
3. sabía
4. conocían
5. pedían
6. corríamos
7. partías
8. pasaba
9. esperabais
10. acababan
11. caminaba
12. comprendía
13. tomaban
14. escribía
15. amaba
16. conocíais
17. bebías
18. comprábamos
19. subían
20. corría
21. respondía
22. guardabas
23. aprendía
24. llevaban
25. pasabais

B.
1. contestábamos, we were answering
2. vendías, you were selling
3. preguntaba, he was asking
4. aprendía, I was learning
5. escuchaban, they were listening
6. Ud. escribía, you were writing
7. aprendían, they were learning
8. Ud. estudiaba, you were studying
9. vivíamos, we were living
10. temía, he was fearing
11. abría, he was opening
12. enseñaban, they were teaching
13. asistía, he was attending
14. tomábamos, we were taking
15. leía, I was reading
16. Uds. bebían, you were drinking
17. temía, I was fearing
18. recibían, they were receiving
19. necesitaba, I was needing
20. Uds. vivían, you were living
21. abríamos, we were opening
22. contestabais, you were answering
23. tomabas, you were taking
24. bebía, he was drinking
25. abrías, you were opening

Mastery Test

pp. 11–12

1. vivían
2. trabajábamos
3. no vendías
4. vivíamos
5. no necesitaban
6. Ud. aprendía
7. creía
8. preguntabais
9. temía
10. ¿comprendías?
11. enseñaba
12. Uds. tomaban
13. no escuchábamos
14. vendía
15. Uds. abrían
16. ¿recibían?
17. asistíamos
18. estudiabas
19. leía
20. vivían
21. Uds. no escondían
22. recibía
23. no comprendían
24. comía
25. Ud. vendía
26. no tomabas
27. escuchaban
28. ¿asistía?
29. necesitabais
30. contestaba

3 PRETERIT

Para practicar

pp. 13–15

viajé, trabajé, estudié, comí, vendí, insistí, recibí.

uniste, acabaste, compraste, rompiste, corriste, abriste, tomaste.

comió, asistió, echó, preparó, subió, pasó, trabajó.

viajó, habló, aprendió, resistió, llamó, respondió, echó.

trabajamos, compramos, amamos, vendimos, bebimos, corrimos, vivimos.

estudiasteis, comisteis, abristeis, tomasteis, viajasteis, subisteis, pasasteis.

trabajaron, compraron, hablaron, aprendieron, temieron, escribieron, viajaron.

guardaron, comprendieron, asistieron, abrieron, pasaron, echaron, bebieron.

Aplicación

pp. 15–16

A.
1. llevé
2. abrimos
3. llegaste
4. comieron
5. bebió
6. metisteis
7. viajaron
8. vivió
9. pasaron
10. vendieron
11. abrí
12. asistió
13. recibieron
14. tomamos
15. temisteis
16. abrió
17. escribieron
18. necesitaron
19. vendiste
20. bebimos
21. aprendieron
22. tomé
23. estudió
24. bebió
25. recibí

B.
1. tomamos, tomábamos
2. enseñaron, enseñaban
3. contestó, contestaba
4. recibieron, recibían
5. aprendió, aprendía
6. asistí, asistía
7. temimos, temíamos
8. vendieron, vendían
9. aprendí, aprendía
10. contesté, contestaba
11. tomaron, tomaban
12. abrió, abría
13. necesitó, necesitaba
14. recibiste, recibías
15. trabajó, trabajaba
16. echaron, echaban
17. subieron, subían
18. comprendí, comprendía
19. corrió, corría
20. trabajé, trabajaba
21. preparó, preparaba
22. guardaron, guardaban
23. pasamos, pasábamos
24. viajé, viajaba
25. echaste, echabas

Mastery Test

pp. 16–17

1. contestamos
2. vendieron
3. aprendí
4. ¿escuchaste?
5. no preguntó
6. Ud. escondió
7. tomamos
8. no bebieron
9. asistimos
10. enseñé
11. preguntaste
12. trabajaron
13. Uds. unieron
14. viví
15. contestasteis
16. Uds. escribieron
17. comprendió
18. no aprendieron
19. escribimos
20. ¿estudió?
21. vendiste
22. enseñó
23. asistió
24. vendí
25. vivisteis
26. recibieron
27. asistí
28. preguntaron
29. bebimos
30. Ud. estudió
31. no contesté
32. ¿abrieron Uds.?
33. no comprendieron
34. no necesitaste
35. vendimos
36. ¿tomó Ud.?
37. no recibimos
38. temió
39. escribí
40. ¿preguntasteis?

Repaso (Present, imperfect, preterit)

pp. 18–19

1. vivían
2. abría
3. no trabajaron
4. subíamos
5. comprendo
6. no tomaron
7. corría
8. contestaron
9. trabajo
10. preparaste
11. Uds. estudiaban
12. guardan
13. pasábamos
14. viajé
15. Ud. necesita
16. no vivía
17. Uds. abrían
18. escribía
19. subo
20. comprendió
21. escribía
22. respondes
23. comprendimos
24. no aprendisteis
25. preparan
26. aprendemos
27. corrimos
28. Uds. pasaban
29. trabajaron
30. asistimos
31. no escribíamos
32. eché
33. estudiábamos
34. trabajé
35. vivíamos
36. guardamos
37. comprendiste
38. asistieron
39. vendíamos
40. paso
41. viví
42. temes
43. escuchó
44. no guardasteis
45. bebe
46. guardaban
47. partió
48. Ud. temió
49. subimos
50. no contesto

4 FUTURE

Para practicar

pp. 20–22

compraré, hablaré, leeré, viviré, sentiré, seré, asistiré.

estudiarás, encontrarás, correrás, tomarás, venderás, conocerás, partirás.

enseñará, perderá, dormirá, aprenderá, recibirá, abrirá, necesitará.

dudará, creerá, amará, escribirá, guardará, correrá, subirá.

contestaremos, temeremos, preguntaremos, subiremos, viajaremos, aprenderemos, viviremos.

prepararéis, echaréis, contestaréis, trabajaréis, viajaréis, responderéis, amaréis.

comprarán, leerán, sentirán, recibirán, decidirán, andarán, pasarán.

prepararán, aprenderán, echarán, viajarán, contestarán, correrán, marcharán.

Aplicación

pp. 22–23

A.
1. hablará
2. estaremos
3. será
4. encontrarán
5. leerá
6. dudaré
7. perderemos
8. enseñarás
9. dormiréis
10. andará
11. decidirás
12. compraré
13. vivirá
14. sentirá
15. beberá
16. estudiaréis
17. abrirá
18. venderás
19. escucharán
20. aprenderán
21. necesitará
22. contestará
23. temeremos
24. tomaré
25. recibirás

B.
1. vivirán,
   they will live
2. abriré,
   I will open
3. subiremos,
   we will go up
4. comprenderás
   you will understand
5. aprenderemos,
   we will learn
6. trabajarán
   they will work
7. Ud. correrá,
   you will run
8. contestarán,
   they will answer
9. trabajaré,
   I will work
10. prepararéis,
    you will prepare
11. pasaremos,
    we will spend
12. viajaré,
    I will travel
13. echarás,
    you will throw
14. partiré,
    I will leave
15. abriréis,
    you will open
16. Uds. escribirán,
    you will write

17. subiré,
I will go up
18. comprenderá,
she will understand
19. correremos,
we will run
20. Ud. contestará,
you will answer
21. tomaremos,
we will take

22. enseñarán,
they will teach
23. acabarás,
you will finish
24. trabajará,
he will work
25. escribiré
I will write

Mastery Test

pp. 24–25

1. adornarás
2. admiraba
3. ofenderéis
4. molesta
5. Uds. discutirán
6. insistí
7. discutirá
8. emprenderemos
9. limpiarán
10. Uds. llaman
11. admiraré
12. adornó
13. molestas
14. discutiré
15. insistieron
16. cubrían
17. cubriremos
18. admiramos
19. Uds. emprendieron
20. insistimos

21. discutieron
22. limpiaremos
23. limpiaba
24. decidí
25. llama
26. ofendíamos
27. llamaremos
28. Ud. discutió
29. no admiraremos
30. no llaman
31. decidís
32. cubrí
33. Ud. no discutirá
34. no decidiremos
35. ¿limpiarás?
36. no insistiréis
37. cubrirán
38. Uds. limpiaron
39. insistíamos
40. ofendió

CONDITIONAL

Para practicar

pp. 26–28

admiraría, decidiría, trabajaría, viviría, bebería, abriría, moriría.

adornarías, ofenderías, responderías, estudiarías, venderías, escribirías, sentirías.

molestaría, emprendería, correría, necesitaría, aprendería, llevaría, partiría.

Para practicar (*cont.*)

llamaría, echaría, aprendería, contestaría, temería, sacaría, hablaría.

limpiaríamos, viajaríamos, comprenderíamos, preguntaríamos, leeríamos, tocaríamos, comeríamos.

cubriríais, pasaríais, subiríais, enseñaríais, creeríais, conoceríais, meteríais.

discutirían, guardarían, abrirían, escucharían, recibirían, traerían, pedirían.

insistirían, prepararían, escribirían, tomarían, asistirían, dormirían, rogarían.

Aplicación

pp. 28–29

A.
1. admirarían
2. discutiría
3. cubrirías
4. limpiaría
5. venderíais
6. preguntaría
7. venderían
8. estudiaríamos
9. viviríamos
10. temería
11. abriría
12. tomarían
13. escribiríamos
14. contestarían
15. temerían
16. llevarías
17. bebería
18. aprendería
19. echaría
20. viajarían
21. necesitaríais
22. escucharían
23. enseñaríamos
24. asistirían
25. recibirías

B. a)
1. contestaríamos, we should answer
2. aprendería, I should learn
3. escucharían, they should listen
4. leería, he should read
5. esconderíamos, we should hide
6. escribiríais, you should write
7. estudiarían, you should study
8. vendería, I should sell
9. enseñaría, she should teach
10. comprenderían, they should understand

b)
1. vivirían, you should live
2. abriría, he should open
3. trabajarían, they should work
4. subiríamos, we should go up
5. comprendería, he should understand
6. aprenderíais, you should learn
7. correría, he should run
8. prepararías, you should prepare
9. guardaríamos, we should keep
10. viajaría, she should travel

Mastery Test

pp. 29–30

1. decidirás
2. molestaría
3. Ud. adornaba
4. ¿ofendería?
5. insistí
6. discutiríamos
7. admiraron
8. no adornaría
9. no ofenderé
10. ofendían
11. ¿limpiaría?
12. emprenden
13. admirarían
14. limpiaré
15. Uds. molestarían
16. no cubriremos
17. cubre
18. decidirían
19. ¿admirarás?
20. admiramos
21. insistían
22. no insistiría
23. Uds. limpiaron
24. decidiría
25. insistirás
26. ¿llamarían?
27. cubriríais
28. molestaremos
29. no ofenderían
30. ¿decidiré?

6 PROGRESSIVE TENSES

Para practicar

p. 32

admirando, adornando, subiendo, cubriendo, acabando, corriendo, respondiendo, tomando, sacando, decidiendo, dando.

estoy abriendo, estoy llevando, estoy perdiendo, estoy buscando, estoy estudiando, estoy bebiendo.

estás viviendo, estás aprendiendo, estás tomando, estás escribiendo, estás trabajando, estás enseñando.

están vendiendo, están abriendo, están contestando, están asistiendo, están escuchando, están entrando.

estamos recibiendo, estamos echando, estamos admirando, estamos pasando, estamos respondiendo, estamos corriendo.

Aplicación

pp. 32–33

A.
1. estaba llevando
2. estabas estudiando
3. estabais trabajando
4. estábamos subiendo
5. estaban corriendo
6. estaba escuchando
7. estaban jugando
8. estábamos escribiendo
9. estabas comiendo
10. estaba partiendo
11. estábamos tomando
12. estaban acabando
13. estaba respondiendo
14. estaban decidendo
15. estaba cubriendo

B.
1. están recibiendo
2. estábamos trabajando
3. estáis abriendo
4. estabais preguntando
5. no estaba escuchando
6. estamos viviendo
7. está bebiendo
8. estaban asistiendo
9. estás vendiendo
10. no estaba tomando
11. estaba enseñando
12. estáis contestando
13. está estudiando
14. no estaba comiendo
15. estoy aprendiendo

170

Mastery Test

pp. 33–34

1. admiraba,	estaba admirando
2. decides,	estás decidiendo
3. limpiaba,	estaba limpiando
4. insistían,	estaban insistiendo
5. si no preparan,	no están preparando
6. Ud. llama,	Ud. está llamando
7. cubrían,	estaban cubriendo
8. ¿adornaban Uds.?,	¿estaban adornando Uds.?
9. si bebe,	está bebiendo
10. vivíamos,	estábamos viviendo
11. no escribías,	no estabas escribiendo
12. paso,	estoy pasando
13. si estudian,	están estudiando
14. pasábamos,	estábamos pasando
15. ¿subís?	¿estáis subiendo?
16. abría,	estaba abriendo
17. ¿corría?,	¿estaba corriendo?
18. no vivía,	no estaba viviendo
19. no escribimos,	no estamos escribiendo

Repaso (Future, conditional, progressive)

pp. 34–35

1. Uds. asistirán
2. estaba admirando
3. ofenderás
4. molestaría
5. estáis buscando
6. Ud. no discutiría
7. estaba insistiendo
8. está estudiando
9. subiré
10. admiraría
11. estaban respondiendo
12. no está molestando
13. ¿discutirán?
14. estaba trabajando
15. no estás corriendo
16. escuchará
17. estaba entrando
18. estamos pasando
19. cubriríamos
20. estaban limpiando
21. no abriré
22. perderíais
23. Ud. está llamando
24. limpiará
25. enseñarás
26. estáis trabajando
27. echará
28. estaba escribiendo
29. están bebiendo
30. admiraría
31. estábamos llamando
32. estaba discutiendo
33. admiraré
34. Ud. molestaría
35. pasarán
36. Uds. escribirían
37. estaban decidiendo
38. responderá

7 PERFECT TENSES

pp. 36–37

tú habías hablado, Ud. había hablado, él había hablado, nosotros habíamos hablado, vosotros habíais hablado, Uds. habían hablado, ellos habían hablado.

yo habré comido, tú habrás comido, Ud. habrá comido, él habrá comido, nosotros habremos comido, vosotros habréis comido, Uds. habrán comido, ellos habrán comido.

I will have eaten, you will have eaten, he will have eaten, we will have eaten, you will have eaten, they will have eaten.

yo habría partido, tú habrías partido, Ud. habría partido, él habría partido, nosotros habríamos partido, vosotros habríais partido, Uds. habrían partido, ellos habrían partido.

I would have left, you would have left, he would have left, we would have left, you would have left, they would have left.

Para practicar

pp. 37–38

1. he aprendido, había aprendido, habré aprendido, habría aprendido
2. han limpiado, habían limpiado, habrán limpiado, habrían limpiado
3. ha vivido, había vivido, habrá vivido, habría vivido
4. hemos comprado, habíamos comprado, habremos comprado, habríamos comprado
5. has asistido, habías asistido, habrás asistido, habrías asistido
6. han vendido, habían vendido, habrán vendido, habrían vendido
7. hemos tomado, habíamos tomado, habremos tomado, habríamos tomado
8. ha aprendido, había aprendido, habrá aprendido, habría aprendido
9. ha bebido, había bebido, habrá bebido, habría bedido
10. ha contestado, había contestado, habrá contestado, habría contestado
11. habéis recibido, habíais recibido, habréis recibido, habríais recibido
12. han preparado, habían preparado, habrán preparado, habrían preparado
13. hemos enseñado, habíamos enseñado, habremos enseñado, habríamos enseñado
14. has temido, habías temido, habrás temido, habrías temido
15. ha preguntado, había preguntado, habrá preguntado, habría preguntado
16. han estudiado, habían estudiado, habrán estudiado, habrían estudiado
17. ha pasado, había pasado, habrá pasado, habría pasado
18. hemos subido, habíamos subido, habremos subido, habríamos subido
19. han salido, habían salido, habrán salido, habrían salido
20. has guardado, habías guardado, habrás guardado, habrías guardado
21. he esperado, había esperado, habré esperado, habría esperado
22. habéis trabajado, habíais trabajado, habréis trabajado, habríais trabajado
23. han vivido, habían vivido, habrán vivido, habrían vivido
24. ha partido, había partido, habrá partido, habría partido
25. ha acabado, había acabado, habrá acabado, habría acabado

172

Aplicación

p. 39

1. Ud. ha comprendido
2. habías vendido
3. habían escuchado
4. habrán subido
5. ha preguntado
6. Ud. habrá discutido
7. habían aprendido
8. Ud. había estudiado
9. has escrito
10. habremos guardado
11. habrían admirado
12. habréis echado
13. habías temido
14. he asistido
15. habíamos tomado
16. habrías preparado
17. había bebido
18. habremos vivido
19. hemos corrido
20. habrá viajado
21. habrías decidido
22. habíais contestado
23. habíais partido
24. habré limpiado
25. habríais molestado

Mastery Test

pp. 39–40

1. habré aprendido
2. había limpiado
3. hemos comprado
4. habían vivido
5. habría corrido
6. he preguntado
7. habrás recibido
8. habías temido
9. ha asistido
10. habrían vendido
11. habremos tomado
12. Ud. ha contestado
13. he necesitado
14. Uds. habrían preguntado
15. han pasado
16. habrás discutido
17. han recibido
18. habría decidido
19. habrán escuchado
20. habremos entrado
21. Ud. habría asistido
22. habíais comprendido
23. hemos vivido
24. Uds. habrán trabajado
25. había tomado

Repaso (Indicative tenses)

pp. 40–41

1. contestas
2. vivían
3. estaba abriendo
4. estáis vendiendo
5. admiraré
6. trabajaron
7. si pregunta
8. Uds. no ofenderán
9. subíamos
10. si no venden
11. molestaría
12. estaba comprendiendo
13. estudiamos
14. ¿estáis adornando?
15. Uds. estaban aprendiendo
16. no vivimos
17. Ud. discute
18. estaba corriendo

19. ¿necesita?
20. molestaron
21. no contestaron
22. teme
23. insistimos
24. trabajé
25. echaré
26. preparabais
27. si abre
28. Ud. estaba admirando
29. guardaron
30. ofenderé
31. estábamos pasando
32. adornaría
33. limpiaremos
34. escribimos

35. estaban cubriendo
36. Uds. estaban echando
37. temerán
38. estaba viviendo
39. viajaba
40. estudias
41. Uds. están llamando
42. abriríais
43. si bebo
44. estábamos insistiendo
45. escribías
46. ¿llamarán?
47. subí
48. no discutirían
49. comprendió
50. viven

8 PRESENT SUBJUNCTIVE

Para practicar

pp. 42–44

eche, aprenda, moleste, emprenda, comprenda, asista, viva.

viajes, comprendas, llames, estudies, bebas, abras, escribas.

pase, suba, limpie, necesite, venda, escriba, prepare.

guarde, abra, cubra, conteste, aprenda, llame, tome.

preparemos, escribamos, discutamos, preguntemos, temamos, trabajemos, unamos.

trabajéis, viváis, insistáis, enseñéis, leáis, paséis, temáis.

respondan, admiren, decidan, escuchen, vivan, guarden, viajen.

corran, adornen, ofendan, tomen, reciban, echen, suban.

Aplicación

pp. 44–45

A.
1. lleve
2. viva
3. escriban
4. trabajéis
5. lean
6. hable
7. Ud. estudie
8. llamemos
9. viajes
10. abra
11. creamos
12. mande
13. escribas
14. tomemos
15. comprendan
16. coma
17. vivas
18. asista
19. Ud. note
20. caminen
21. meta
22. observéis
23. partáis
24. andes
25. insistamos

Aplicación (*cont.*)

B.
1. comprendas
2. lea
3. reciba
4. vendan
5. coma
6. cante
7. estudie
8. beban
9. tomemos
10. viváis
11. enseñe
12. corran

Mastery Test

pp. 45–46

A.
1. Es posible que ella no entienda
2. Ojalá que estudies
3. ¡Qué recibamos…!
4. Es posible que viva
5. Ojalá que vendan
6. ¡Qué trabajen!
7. Ojalá que aprendáis
8. Es posible que enseñemos
9. Ojalá que asista
10. Es posible que recibas

B.
1. si estudia
2. ojalá que estudie
3. si vende
4. ojalá que no venda
5. si aprende
6. ojalá que aprenda
7. si vivimos
8. ojalá que vivamos
9. si asisten
10. ojalá que asistan

9 IMPERATIVE

Para practicar

pp. 47–48

viaja, trabaja, estudia, come, vende, insiste.

partid, corred, trabajad, recibid, estudiad, comprad.

no unas, no acabes, no compres, no rompas, no abras, no corras.

no toméis, no asistéis, no preparéis, no bebáis, no temáis.

Para practicar

p. 48

trabaje, no asista, conteste, no cante, abra, coma.

no corran, lleven, no metan, no teman, tomen, comprendan.

no tomemos, estudiemos, no contestemos, comamos, no vendamos, preparemos.

Aplicación

pp. 49–50

A.
1. lleva
2. corred
3. no coman
4. trabajemos
5. no abras
6. no teman
7. compre
8. no prepares
9. viaja
10. vendamos
11. no asistáis
12. asistamos
13. escuchen
14. cocina
15. no enseñe
16. no contestes
17. echad
18. suban

B.
1. no vendas
2. comed
3. no beban
4. escribe
5. no compréis
6. compremos
7. no estudiemos
8. corran
9. contesta
10. llame
11. comprended
12. asistan
13. preguntemos
14. enseña
15. no abras
16. viajad
17. respondan
18. suba

10 IMPERFECT SUBJUNCTIVE

Para practicar

p. 52

temiera, asistiera, abriera, acabara, escuchara, necesitara.

estudiara, abriera, aprendiera, tuviera, hablara, enseñara.

comprendiéramos, comiéramos, entráramos, partiéramos, viviéramos, metiéramos.

partieses, preguntases, vivieses, vendieses, hablases, guardases.

enseñase, tomase, comiese, aprendiese, asistiese, pasase.

hablasen, contestasen, estudiasen, tomasen, leyesen, escribiesen.

Aplicación

p. 53

A.
1. hablara, hablase
2. viviéramos, viviésemos
3. corriéramos, corriésemos
4. partieras, partieses
5. pasara, pasase
6. esperarais, esperaseis
7. acabaran, acabasen
8. caminara, caminase
9. comprendiera, comprendiese
10. tomaran, tomasen
11. escribiera, escribiese
12. amara, amase
13. bebieras, bebieses
14. compráramos, comprásemos
15. subieran, subiesen

176

Aplicación (*cont.*)

B.
1. contestáramos, contestásemos
2. vendieras, vendieses
3. preguntara, preguntase
4. aprendiera, aprendiese
5. escucharan, escuchasen
6. Ud. escribiera, escribiese
7. aprendieran, aprendiesen
8. Ud. estudiara, estudiase
9. viviéramos, viviésemos
10. temiera, temiese
11. abriera, abriese
12. enseñaran, enseñasen
13. asistiera, asistiese
14. tomáramos, tomásemos
15. Uds. recibieran, recibiesen

Para practicar

pp. 53–54

1. escuchara
2. comieran
3. no discutieran
4. entraras
5. abriera
6. comprendieras
7. practicara
8. cantara
9. escuchareis
10. abrieran
11. gastaran
12. aprendiéramos
13. ganara
14. no llamara
15. escribiérais

Mastery Test 1

pp. 54–55

1. si yo enseñara
2. si ellos vivieran
3. si subiéramos
4. si yo no comprendiera
5. si ellos tomaran
6. si él corriera
7. si tú contestaras
8. si yo trabajara
9. si vosotros no prepararéis
10. si Ud. estudiara
11. si ellos guardaran
12. si nosotros no gastáramos
13. si yo viajara
14. si tú necesitaras
15. si yo no viviera
16. si vosotros abriráis
17. si ella escribiera
18. si Uds. respondieran
19. si él temiera
20. si ellos comieran

Mastery Test 2

p. 55

1. era posible que ellos asistieran
2. era imposible que él cantara
3. ojalá que tú llamara
4. si ella estudiara
5. si ellos trabajaran
6. era imposible que él limpiara
7. ojalá que hablaras
8. si vosotros vendierais
9. era posible que vosotros recibierais
10. ojalá que ellos contestaran

11 PERFECT TENSES OF THE SUBJUNCTIVE

Para practicar

p. 58

haya estudiado, haya necesitado, haya viajado,

hayamos pasado, hayas tomado, hayan vendido,

hayáis asistido, hayan llamado, hubiera (hubiese) vivido, hubieran (hubiesen) guardado, hubieras (hubieses)

caminado,

hubieran (hubiesen) bebido, hubiéramos (hubiésemos) echado,

hubierais (hubieseis) asistido, hubiera (hubiese) aprendido

Aplicación

p. 58

1. haya escuchado
2. hayan trabajado
3. hayamos comprendido
4. haya comprendido
5. hay corrido
6. no hayas preparado
7. hayamos pasado
8. hayáis viajado
9. hayan necesitado
10. haya subido
11. no hayas aprendido
12. no haya vivido
13. hubiéramos vivido
14. hubieran guardado
15. hubiéramos vivido
16. hubieras subido
17. no hubiera tomado
18. hubieron respondido
19. hubieras estudiado
20. hubiera partido
21. hubieras temido
22. hubieran asistido
23. no hubiera contestado
24. hubieras discutido

Mastery Test

p. 59

1. si yo hubiera aprendido
2. era posible que él hubiera tomado
3. si ella hubiera limpiado
4. es imposible que tú hayas trabajado
5. ojalá que hubiéramos comprado
6. si hubiéramos vivido
7. ojalá que ellos hubieran recibido
8. si vosotros hubiérais comprendido
9. ojalá que ella hubiera asistido
10. es imposible que hayamos tomado
11. si yo necesitara
12. si ud. hubiera preguntado
13. es posible que ellos no hayan salido
14. ojalá que ella hubiera ganado
15. ojalá que ella haya entrado
16. si yo hubiera preguntado
17. ojalá que ellos hubieran escuchado
18. ojalá que vosotros no hayan temido
19. si ella hubiera decidido
20. ojalá que vosotros hubieran contestado

Repaso del subjuntivo

p. 60

1. es posible que tú escribas
2. es imposible que tú hayas escrito
3. si tú escribieras
4. ojalá que tú escribas
5. ¡escribe!
6. ojalá que tú hayas escrito
7. ojalá que tú escribieras
8. ojalá que tú hubieras escrito
9. si él asistiera
10. era imposible que ella comprendiera

11. es posible que ellos hayan discutido
12. ojalá que comas
13. ojalá que Uds hayan contestado
14. si viajáramos
15. ojalá que vosotros hayáis leído
16. si ellos corrieran
17. es posible que ella hable
18. qué Uds. insistan
19. ¡qué vivamos en paz!
20. era imposible que ella contestara

12 REFLEXIVE VERBS

pp. 61–63

te levantabas, Ud. se levantaba, él se levantaba, nosotros nos levantábamos, vosotros os levantabais, Uds. se levantaban, ellos se levantaban.

te levantaste, Ud. se levantó, él se levantó, nos levantamos, os levantasteis, Uds. se levantaron, ellos se levantaron.

te levantarás, Ud. se levantará, él se levantará, nos levantaremos, os levantaréis, Uds. se levantarán, ellos se levantarán.

te levantarías, Ud. se levantaría, él se levantaría, nos levantaríamos, os levantaríais, Uds. se levantarían, ellos se levantarían.

me estaba levantando, estaba levantándome; I was getting up

(1) me había levantado (2) me habré levantado (3) me habría levantado

(1) I had gotten up (2) I will have gotten up (3) I would have gotten up

te levantes, Ud. se levante, él se levante, nos levantemos, os levantéis, Uds. se levanten, ellos se levanten

te levantaras, se levantara, se levantara, nos levantáramos, os levantarais, Uds. se levantaran, ellos se levantaran

te levantases, se levantase, se levantase, nos levantásemos, os levantaseis, Uds. se levantasen, ellos se levantasen

me haya levantado, te hayas levantado, se haya levantado, se haya levantado

I may have gotten up, you may have gotten up, you may have gotten up, he may have gotten up

nos hubiésemos levantado, os hubieseis levantado, se hubiesen levantado, se hubiesen levantado

we might have gotten up, you might have gotten up, you might have gotten up, they might have gotten up

Aplicación

pp. 63–64

A.
1. os lavéis
2. se peinaban
3. se levantó
4. nos peinemos
5. nos levantábamos
6. se lavan
7. nos levantamos
8. se hayan peinado
9. te lavabas
10. me peiné
11. os levantáis
12. te hubieras levantado
13. se peina
14. me lavaré
15. te peinarías

B.
1. se hayan levantado
2. nos hemos levantado
3. te has peinado
4. os habéis levantado
5. nos habremos peinado
6. me había peinado
7. se había levantado
8. nos habríamos levantado
9. se habían peinado
10. se haya lavado
11. os hayáis peinado
12. nos hayamos lavado
13. me haya levantado
14. se habrán levantado
15. me habré lavado

Mastery Test

pp. 64–65

1. ojalá que se haya lavado
2. se estaban lavando (estaban lavándose)
3. se peinan
4. era posible que él se lavara
5. me había levantado
6. se levantaron
7. se habrán lavado
8. me estoy peinando (estoy peinándome)
9. se habrían levantado
10. me levantaba
11. me lavo
12. es posible que ella se levante
13. nos lavaremos
14. se ha lavado
15. era imposible que nos peináramos
16. se lavaron
17. me lavaría
18. se levantan
19. te lavaste
20. era imposible que ellos se lavaran

Repaso de verbos regulares

pp. 65–68

A.
1. acabamos
2. comprendisteis
3. ellos temían
4. necesitaremos
5. partiríais
6. estamos enseñando
7. partís
8. Uds. hablen
9. han enseñado
10. hayáis hablado
11. estaban lavándose
12. habíais vendido
13. ellos hubiesen asistido
14. bebierais
15. habrán preguntado
16. habríais tomado
17. escuchan
18. hemos estudiado
19. habréis temido
20. aprenderán

Repaso de verbos regulares (*cont.*)

21. comprendáis
22. están viviendo
23. Uds. habían acabado
24. contestamos
25. Uds. vendiesen

26. habríamos partido
27. abríais
28. Uds. entrarían
29. estabais comiendo
30. Uds. hayan tomado

B.
1. I leave
2. you wrote
3. you will attend
4. they used to live
5. we would take
6. you taught
7. he is studying
8. we will fear
9. you were opening
10. she would sell
11. you have attended
12. you have eaten
13. they had understood
14. you are listening
15. we will have had

16. I had studied
17. I was getting up
18. you will have spoken
19. if we drank
20. you would have answered
21. you may eat
22. he may write
23. it's impossible that he washed up
24. if we learned
25. if you had studied
26. I hope you spoke
27. if you had eaten
28. they fear
29. you would have carried
30. you used to carry

C.
1. temen
2. hubiera (hubiese) partido
3. comías
4. hayamos hablado
5. ¿hablasteis?
6. partía
7. aprenderemos
8. tomaras (tomases)
9. no escribiría
10. comprendieron
11. estás contestando
12. habrían partido
13. estabais hablando
14. he estudiado
15. ¡no acabéis!
16. habían partido
17. habré enseñado
18. Ud. habrá vivido
19. estamos viviendo
20. Uds. habrían enseñado
21. temamos
22. no lees
23. vendiera (vendiese)
24. no hayáis comido
25. estaba vendiendo

26. no hubierais (hubieseis) escuchado
27. vendo
28. ¿leerás?
29. llevaban
30. escribiste
31. asistiréis
32. tomaríamos
33. no está estudiando
34. estabais abriendo
35. Ud. no ha asistido
36. había comprendido
37. llevarías
38. habrán estudiado
39. Uds. no habrían necesitado
40. ¡beban!
41. no asistiéramos (asistiésemos)
42. has vivido
43. haya acabado
44. Uds. hubieran (hubiesen) aprendido
45. ¿abrís?
46. temía
47. habías tomado
48. preguntaron
49. Ud. entrará
50. ¿leerías?

13 STEM-CHANGING VERBS—CLASS I

p. 70

(1) piense, peinses, piense, piense, pensemos, penséis, piensen, piensen,

(2) entienda, entiendas, entienda, entienda, entendamos, entendáis, entiendan, entiendan.

(1) cuento, cuentas, cuenta, cuenta, contamos, contáis, cuentan, cuentan,

(2) vuelvo, vuelves, vuelve, vuelve, volvemos, volvéis, vuelven, vuelven.

Para practicar

pp. 70–71

A.

cierro, encuentro, muestro, pierdo, revuelvo, enciendo.

confiesan, se acuestan, mueven, devuelven, aciertan, acuerdan.

nos sentamos, contamos, mostramos, perdemos, devolvemos, entendemos.

B.

cuentes, pienses, muerdas, apruebes, devuelvas, entiendas.

cierren, encuentren, muestren, pierdan, muevan, enciendan.

entendáis, revolváis, mostréis, mováis, conteséis, acordéis.

Mastery Test

p. 72

A.
1. they go to bed
2. I remember
3. she returns
4. you may warm
5. we may show
6. you lose
7. that you will return
8. you may light
9. he approved
10. I used to sit
11. it cost
12. it will snow
13. I confess
14. they give back
15. close

B.
1. perdisteis
2. entiendan
3. nos encontremos
4. ¿cierras?
5. no entiendes
6. movieron
7. estaba moviendo
8. muestren
9. mueves
10. calentamos
11. estoy encendiendo
12. no pierden
13. muerda
14. revuelvas
15. cuesta

14 STEM-CHANGING VERBS—CLASS II

Para practicar

pp. 74–75

adviertes, mientes, mueres, hieres, consientes

se divierta, sienta, duerma, mienta, muera

hirieron, advirtieron, se divirtieron, durmieron, consintieron

muriéramos (muriésemos), sintiéramos (sintiésemos), mintiéramos (mintiésemos), durmiéramos (durmiésemos), advirtiéramos (advirtiésemos)

muriendo, hiriendo, consintiendo, advirtiendo, divirtiéndose

Mastery Test

pp. 75–76

A.
1. you used to lie
2. we sleep (slept)
3. she died
4. if they lied
5. he had felt
6. they have fun
7. he wounded
8. it's impossible that he will spoil
9. I do not notice
10. if he slept
11. I felt
12. I hope you sleep
13. you may feel
14. they may sleep
15. we may have fun

B.
1. no hieren
2. has dormido
3. es posible que consintamos
4. si yo muriera
5. ojalá que duerma
6. te divertiste
7. mentiremos
8. estaban muriendo
9. estaba sintiendo
10. si durmiera
11. consentiría
12. Ud. advirtió
13. duermo
14. si sintieran
15. ojalá que os divirtáis

15 STEM-CHANGING VERBS—CLASS III

Para practicar

pp. 77–78

impide, compite, sirve, mide

gimáis, pidáis, impidáis, compitáis

se vistieron, sirvieron, midieron, impidieron.

Mastery Test

p. 78

1. that they would groan
2. that I will dress
3. he would ask for
4. we used to measure
5. you may measure
6. we prevent
7. you groaned
8. I will compete
9. if we served
10. he groans
11. you measured
12. they served
13. I compete
14. they get dressed
15. that you will prevent

Repaso (Stem-changing verbs)

pp. 78–79

A.

gime, compite, cierra, siente, impide, muestra, encuentra, se divierte, se sienta, revuelve.

B.

aprobemos, midamos, durmamos, confesemos, mintamos, advirtamos, pidamos, nos vistamos, repitamos, consintamos.

C.

1. entienden
2. que consintamos
3. que me vista
4. no se está divirtiendo (no está divirtiéndose)
5. que cerremos
6. pediste
7. no advirtió
8. encuentra
9. que tú gimieras
10. que yo muera
11. que tú muevas
12. que sirviéramos
13. advierten
14. cierro
15. compite
16. que tú muestres
17. que yo me divirtiera
18. sirvieron
19. no perdéis
20. que ella duerma
21. impide
22. que yo devuelva
23. sintieron
24. que Uds. impidan
25. ¿entiende?
26. no están muriendo (no mueren)
27. no compitió
28. que nieve
29. estás mintiendo (mientes)
30. que ellos pidieran

16 ORTHOGRAPHIC CHANGES

Para practicar

pp. 82–83

seques, coloques, obligues, entregues, amenaces, analices, averigües, mengües.

alcancen, abracen, lleguen, castiguen, arriesguen, rasquen, repliquen, expliquen.

expliqué, saqué, indiqué, negué, llegué, castigué, rogué, repliqué, empecé, crucé, rechacé, almorcé, marqué, apacigüé, santigüé.

Mastery Test

pp. 83–84

A.
1. that he will explain
2. if you marked
3. that I will turn off
4. I embraced
5. I handed over
6. that we will stumble
7. that they will dry
8. that you will punish
9. that you will reject
10. that you find out
11. that you reply
12. that we load
13. that you threaten
14. I handed in
15. I took out
16. that we will bless
17. that he arrives
18. that you analyze
19. that they will pacify
20. that he reaches (achieves)

B.
1. que apacigüemos
2. pagué
3. que saquen
4. no averigüé
5. que castigues
6. que no coloque
7. arriesgué
8. que fatiguemos
9. que no replique
10. que cruces
11. roguéis
12. indiqué
13. reza
14. que lances
15. que lleguen
16. no expliqué
17. que no analicemos
18. que repliquéis
19. lancé
20. sollocé

Para practicar

p. 86

encojo, dirijo, cojo, exijo, ejerzo, convenzo, esparzo, extingo, delinco, acojo.

extingamos, delincamos, distingamos, escojamos, inflijamos, finjamos, cojamos, esparzamos, ejerzamos, dirijamos.

Aplicación

p. 87

1. I exercise
2. you convinced
3. I will scatter
4. you used to welcome
5. that they distinguish
6. that we pretend
7. you have convinced
8. I will direct
9. he would follow
10. that you will extinguish
11. you used to exercise
12. I demand
13. I followed
14. you extinguished
15. that they will convince
16. I pretended
17. he broke the law
18. that they catch (seize)
19. I extinguish
20. you may break the law

Mastery Test

pp. 87–88

1. si vencieras
2. que inflija
3. distingo
4. ejercimos
5. no exijo
6. que no distingas
7. no convencerá
8. ¿escogerán Uds.? (¿elegirán Uds.?)
9. no extingamos
10. esparcí
11. dirigimos
12. distinguió
13. delinco
14. ejerces
15. que acoja
16. que extingan
17. que no convenzan
18. finjo
19. distinguiréis
20. que no delincas

Para practicar

p. 90

aparezcas, ofrezcas, merezcas, reconozcas, compadezcas, confíes, guíes, descontinúes.

desafío, parezco, obedezco, agradezco, insinúo, desconfío.

leyeron, poseyeron, enviaron, continuaron, conocieron, ofrecieron.

Aplicación

p. 91

1. estamos leyendo
2. enviáis
3. continuéis
4. ofrecemos
5. Uds. desafíen
6. aborrezcáis
7. merezcamos
8. Uds. aparezcan
9. guiamos
10. desconocieron
11. poseyeron
12. Uds. insinúen
13. se enriquezcan
14. parecimos
15. nos habituamos
16. creyésemos
17. Uds. complacían
18. ellas desconfían
19. descontinuamos
20. reconocemos

Mastery Test

pp. 91–92

1. ¿leyó?
2. es posible que desaparezcamos
3. ojalá que continúe
4. es posible que ellos envíen
5. poseía
6. es posible que Ud. no conozca
7. es posible que desconfiemos
8. no guío
9. es posible que hayan leído
10. es posible que él compadezca
11. enviaba
12. es posible que tú descontinúes
13. creíamos
14. desaparecéis
15. enviaron
16. no creyó
17. aborrecí
18. ¿confías?
19. es imposible que ellos conozcan
20. continuó

17 ORTHOGRAPHIC CHANGES IN STEM-CHANGING VERBS

Para practicar

pp. 95–97

corrijo, ruego, ciego, tropiezo, consigo, construyo, sonrío.

niega, persigue, ríe, destruye, se esfuerza, elige, juega.

colegí, rogué, almorcé, incluí, reí, proseguí, cegué.

corrigieron, consiguieron, sonrieron, restituyeron, eligieron, instruyeron, negaron.

ciegues, juegues, tropieces, corrijas, prosigas, destruyas, rías.

neguemos, nos esforcemos, elijamos, consigamos, sonriamos, concluyamos, juguemos.

corrigiera (corrigiese), prosiguiera (prosiguiese), riera (riese), construyera (construyese), eligiera (eligiese), constituyera (constituyese), consiguiera (consiguiese).

coligiendo, colgando, almorzando, sonriendo, destruyendo, persiguiendo.

cegado, empezado, elegido, seguido, reído, concluido, huido.

Aplicación

pp. 97–98

1. rueguen Uds.
2. tropezamos
3. ellos almuercen
4. cegamos
5. escogemos
6. empezamos
7. juegan
8. nos esforzamos
9. colguéis
10. empezamos
11. huyen
12. Uds. sonrieron
13. ellos destruyeron
14. concluyésemos
15. habéis huido
16. ellos corrijan
17. Uds. consiguieron
18. seguimos
19. escogiéramos
20. consigáis
21. estaban siguiendo
22. elijamos
23. corregimos
24. persiguen
25. incluyáis
26. concluíamos
27. Uds. habían reído
28. instruímos
29. Uds. han restituido
30. están sonriendo

Mastery Test

pp. 98–99

A.
1. that I will turn off
2. I exercise
3. you send
4. I stumble
5. extinguish!
6. I offer
7. I handed over
8. that they will distinguish
9. that you will be unacquainted
10. I played
11. that we will pretend
12. I guide
13. that you will eat lunch
14. I correct
15. he possessed
16. that you will reply
17. that they will catch
18. that you will insinuate
19. that you will threaten
20. I demand
21. that I would believe
22. I marked
23. that you will get
24. I smile
25. that you will beg
26. that they will convince
27. that you would conclude
28. that you will pacify
29. that you will break the law
30. he destroyed

B.
1. pagué
2. que escogiera
3. ¿leyó?
4. no averigüé
5. siguieron
6. ojalá que continúe
7. es posible que no coloque
8. es posible que no extingas
9. ojalá que envíen
10. es posible que lleguemos
11. ¿consiguió Ud.?
12. es posible que no conozcas
13. es posible que cruces
14. sigo
15. no guío
16. rogué
17. delinco
18. es posible que leas
19. ojalá que empecéis
20. es posible que dirija
21. destruyeron
22. no expliqué
23. finjo
24. no te ríes
25. ojalá que repliques
26. es posible que no convenzan
27. creíamos
28. lancé
29. es posible que escojas (elijas)
30. si concluyéramos

Repaso general 1

pp. 100–101

A.
1. partimos
2. comprendisteis
3. vivían
4. asistiremos
5. tomaríais
6. estamos escribiendo
7. estaban vistiéndose
8. hemos hablado
9. Uds. habían vendido
10. habréis asistido
11. habrían bebido
12. contesten Uds.
13. aprendierais
14. hayan entrado
15. hubiéramos tomado

B.
1. temen
2. bebías
3. ojalá que mostréis
4. empecé
5. ¿hablaste?
6. sirvieron
7. creíamos
8. si creyais
9. no escribiría
10. advierte
11. es posible que no convenzan
12. es posible que no empiece
13. hablabas
14. nieva
15. ojalá que expliquen

Repaso general 1 (*cont.*)

16. acordamos
17. se acuesten
18. consintamos
19. no se divierten
20. Uds. pidieron
21. leyeron
22. reímos
23. negamos
24. Uds. incluyan
25. juguéis
26. reconocemos
27. Uds. persiguieron
28. almorcéis
29. averigüemos
30. distinguimos

16. es posible que dirijan
17. habré enseñado
18. si pidieran
19. no te ríes
20. no guío
21. temamos
22. escojo
23. ¿continúas?
24. no expliqué
25. vendía
26. rogué
27. destruyeron
28. es posible que escojas
29. llevaban
30. envía

Repaso general 2

pp. 101–103

A.
1. había temido
2. he partido
3. habían vivido
4. habré necesitado
5. habríamos partido
6. hayas comido
7. hubiésemos vendido
8. Ud. había reído
9. has restituido
10. han enviado
11. he descontinuado
12. he obedecido
13. había creído
14. hayan desaparecido
15. yo hubiera poseído
16. ha tropezado
17. haya distinguido
18. han jugado
19. hayan explicado
20. he conseguido
21. había herido
22. has elegido
23. él haya delinquido
24. han sonreído
25. habían destruido
26. habréis hablado
27. había aprendido
28. había dormido
29. hubiéramos corregido
30. hubiera huido

B.
1. habrían partido
2. ojalá que lean
3. si concluyéramos
4. no está estudiando
5. comprenden
6. pagué
7. ojalá que cruces
8. Ud. llevaría
9. es posible que cerremos
10. era posible que escogiera (eligiera)
11. ¿conseguiste?
12. era imposible que asistiéramos (asistiésemos)
13. si impidieran
14. ¿leyó?
15. lleguemos
16. ¿abre Ud.?
17. impidieron
18. no averigüé
19. no cruzáis
20. entrarás
21. me visto
22. siguieron
23. cierro
24. ¿leerían Uds.?
25. es posible que mueran
26. ¡continúen!
27. sigo
28. Uds. habrán vivido
29. es posible que perdáis
30. es posible que no busque

18 IRREGULAR VERBS

Para practicar

pp. 105–106

desasgo, quepo, ando, decaigo

asen, andan, caen, caben

desasió, cupo, anduvo, cayó

asiremos, decaeremos, cabremos, andaremos

desasgas, caigas, quepas, andes

decayerais (decayeseis), anduvierais (anduvieseis), cupierais (cupieseis), asierais (asieseis)

Aplicación

p. 106

1. they would fall
2. we will fit
3. that you fell/have fallen
4. you were walking
5. you would fit
6. they fell
7. you would decline
8. you fitted
9. we loosen
10. we walked
11. that we will decline
12. that they will fit
13. that you will fall
14. I will seize
15. we declined
16. he will fall
17. that I would fit
18. I fall
19. I fit
20. that they will seize
21. that you would decline
22. we will walk
23. that they seized/would have seized
24. they would have walked
25. you will loosen
26. they are declining
27. that we will walk
28. he will have declined
29. that they walked/would walk
30. you seize

Mastery Test

pp. 107–108

1. que no cayeran
2. que hubiera andado
3. asirían
4. ¿andabas?
5. decaen
6. si desasieran (desasiesen)
7. que decaeríais
8. ¿andaré?
9. desasgo
10. anduvo
11. ¿cupo?
12. desasíamos
13. decayeron
14. habríamos cabido
15. no caeré
16. cabe
17. ojalá que andemos
18. había asido
19. no habría caído
20. ande
21. habías asido
22. ando
23. Uds. caerían
24. ¿asió?
25. ha caído
26. ojalá que quepamos
27. andabas
28. caíamos

Mastery Test *(cont.)*

29. que hayas andado
30. habíamos cabido
31. que haya asido
32. caísteis
33. si hubiera caído
34. Ud. cupo

35. cupiera (cupiese)
36. decaes
37. asgan
38. cayéramos (cayésemos)
39. no quepa
40. caigáis

Para practicar

p. 110

deduzco, maldigo, yerro, doy, traduzco.

produjeron, bendijeron, dieron, condujeron, erraron.

traducirá, maldecirá, deducirá, bendecirá, dará.

habían dado, habían deducido, habían bendecido, habían errado, habían dicho.

des, produzcas, bendigas, yerres, digas.

erráramos (errásemos), tradujéramos (tradujésemos), maldijéramos (maldijésemos), diéramos (diésemos), condujéramos (condujésemos).

Aplicación

pp. 110–111

1. you deduced
2. you give
3. he will say
4. that we will wander
5. we used to lead
6. that they will give
7. that we will say
8. you were cursing
9. he translates
10. you would have given
11. they said
12. that I said/have said
13. she led
14. I give
15. you may wander

16. we would say
17. that I will deduce
18. you gave
19. they bless
20. you wander
21. he would produce
22. that you would give
23. that he would say
24. I wander
25. that she would translate
26. we were giving
27. they would have cursed
28. I wandered
29. I produce
30. I will give

Mastery Test

pp. 111–112

1. dirás
2. conducís
3. erremos
4. es posible que haya dicho
5. no daba
6. tradujiste
7. si bendijera
8. daremos
9. es imposible que produzcan
10. ¿condujo?
11. si hubieras dicho
12. ¿da?
13. yerro
14. es posible que deduzca
15. maldeciríamos
16. dieron
17. si produjera
18. ¡no traduzcan!
19. ¿están diciendo?
20. erraron
21. es posible que hayan dado
22. ¿no habéis dicho?
23. produzco
24. yerra
25. no diremos
26. no decían
27. no doy
28. es posible que deduzca
29. si no tradujeran
30. maldijiste
31. ¿disteis?
32. conduciremos
33. ojalá que den
34. bendigo
35. produjeron
36. traducías
37. es posible que no haya dado
38. es posible que maldiga
39. si no hubieran dado
40. es posible que no conduzca

Para practicar

p. 114

1. vamos
2. Uds. satisfagan
3. habrán
4. estamos
5. ibais
6. nosotros hubiéramos
7. hemos
8. estuvieron
9. fuimos
10. harán
11. hubisteis
12. hicierais
13. ellos vayan
14. estuvierais
15. habéis hecho
16. Uds. hayan
17. fuerais
18. satisficieron
19. Uds. estén
20. satisfacemos

Aplicación

pp. 114–115

1. he will have satisfied
2. we are
3. there is (are)
4. you went
5. he would do
6. you satisfied
7. there would have been
8. that you did/have done
9. I would not be
10. I will satisfy
11. they had
12. we used to do (make)
13. you were going
14. that we satisfied/would satisfy
15. that there were/have been
16. I would have been
17. that you will satisfy
18. that you would be
19. you would have
20. we did

Aplicación (*cont.*)

21. they were
22. that he would do
23. he has
24. that you will not go
25. I would have done

26. you were satisfying
27. that we would go
28. that they are
29. I was
30. he goes

Mastery Test

pp. 115–116

1. que hubiéramos ido
2. estuve
3. que haya hecho
4. habrían satisfecho
5. estaba
6. no habrán ido
7. no hacíamos
8. Uds. satisfarán
9. estamos
10. había hecho
11. iba
12. satisfice
13. ojalá que estemos
14. no hay
15. no satisfacemos
16. ¿va?
17. Ud. estará
18. hicieron
19. ojalá que satisfagamos
20. es posible que no estuviera (estuviese)

21. habría habido
22. si fueras
23. satisfacía
24. habrá
25. es posible que vaya
26. si hubiera (hubiese) habido
27. es imposible que satisfaga
28. harás
29. si hubiera (hubiese)
30. si hubieran (hubiesen) estado
31. fuisteis
32. ha habido
33. ojalá que no hagan
34. satisfago
35. si no hubieran (hubiesen) hecho
36. no iré
37. ojalá que haya
38. haríamos
39. había
40. no estoy

Para practicar

p. 118

propones, hueles, puedes, oyes, compones.

dispusieron, pudieron, oyeron, impusieron, supusieron.

dispondré, expondré, impondré, propondré, supondré.

componga, pueda, oiga, huela, exponga.

hayamos oído, hayamos dispuesto, hayamos puesto, hayamos supuesto, hayamos podido.

Aplicación

pp. 118–119

1. pusieran
2. podamos
3. oirían
4. pudisteis
5. disponéis
6. oíamos
7. Uds. podrán
8. olieron
9. hemos compuesto
10. habremos podido
11. oiremos
12. oleríais
13. impondrían
14. podían
15. habrán oído
16. huelen
17. expongamos
18. oyeron
19. pudiéramos
20. hayamos propuesto
21. podríais
22. oigáis
23. olemos
24. supondréis
25. podéis
26. Uds. oyen
27. oláis
28. dispusieron
29. oliéramos
30. hubierais puesto

Mastery Test

pp. 119–120

1. oíste
2. es posible que huela
3. huela
4. no habría puesto
5. no estabais oyendo (no oíais)
6. están imponiendo
7. pude
8. ¿huele?
9. oirían
10. pueda
11. habré compuesto
12. ¿pone?
13. ¿oye?
14. no expondrás
15. ojalá que propongan
16. no pudiera (pudiese)
17. era posible que oyéramos
18. Uds. podrían
19. era imposible que olieran (oliesen)
20. es posible que supongamos
21. no oiréis
22. ¿puedes?
23. si dispusiéramos
24. no pondrán
25. oyeron
26. pudisteis
27. suponía
28. podrás
29. si no oyéramos
30. ¿expusisteis?

Aplicación

pp. 122–123

A.
1. fuimos (éramos)
2. supieras (supieses)
3. salimos (salíamos)
4. supo (sabía)
5. fuiste (eras)
6. saliera (saliese)
7. fuera (fuese)
8. fui (era)
9. quisimos (queríamos)
10. salí (salía)
11. había sabido
12. habíais salido
13. quiso (quería)
14. estabas saliendo
15. quisieran (quisiesen)

C.
1. we would be
2. we were
3. you wanted
4. I will have been
5. that you would be/were
6. I have known
7. we will have known
8. that we will want
9. you will know
10. you were

B.
1. salíamos
2. Uds. sabrán
3. querréis
4. salieron
5. sepáis
6. saldríais
7. saben
8. sois
9. habíamos querido
10. salgan
11. serán
12. quisieran
13. saldremos
14. seamos
15. Uds. fueran

11. he knew
12. he had gone out
13. they were wanting
14. you would know
15. that they left/have left
16. if we had known
17. if he wanted/would like
18. he might want
19. they might leave
20. if we knew

Mastery Test

pp. 123–124

1. si supiera
2. habéis salido
3. querría
4. no fui
5. habéis sabido
6. somos
7. ojalá que salga
8. querrás
9. sabíamos
10. era
11. queríamos
12. es posible que no salgamos
13. sabréis
14. ojalá que sean
15. es posible que haya querido
16. Ud. no será
17. habrán sabido
18. salieron
19. habías querido
20. no salimos

21. es posible que haya sabido
22. ¿es?
23. salías
24. no quise
25. habrían sabido
26. ¿no quieren?
27. hemos sido
28. saldrá
29. sabríamos
30. si quisieras
31. salgo
32. Ud. supo
33. he querido
34. es posible que hayamos sido
35. es posible que quieras
36. ¿saldrían?
37. sé
38. si fuera
39. fueron
40. habremos sido

Para practicar

p. 126

contraigo, convengo, detengo, mantengo, sostengo.

mantiene, viene, vale, retiene, trae.

convendrán, detendrán, mantendrán, valdrán, sostendrán.

contuvo, trajo, convino, sostuvo, detuvo.

vengas, mantengas, contraigas, contengas, valgas.

contrajéramos (contrajésemos), viniéramos (viniésemos), tuviéramos (tuviésemos), sostuviéramos (sostuviésemos), mantuviéramos (mantuviésemos).

Aplicación

p. 127

1. he will have come
2. that you brought/have brought
3. they had
4. that we are worth
5. they will bring
6. I had
7. we would be worth
8. they had come
9. we used to have
10. you would bring
11. you have been worth
12. you come
13. you will be worth
14. if he came
15. I brought
16. I will have
17. if he were worth
18. that they would have
19. he has brought
20. that they come
21. they used to bring
22. you would have
23. we used to be worth
24. we will have come
25. that you bring
26. you have
27. I would be worth
28. if you had
29. that we brought/would bring
30. you were coming

195

Mastery Test

pp. 127–128

1. no ha vendio
2. había tenido
3. ojalá que traigas
4. valió
5. es posible que hayamos tenido
6. habían traido
7. vinisteis
8. traía
9. tuvo
10. valen
11. no tendrían
12. trajo
13. venían
14. ¿tienes?
15. ojalá que traigan
16. es posible que venga
17. no estamos trayendo
18. tendremos
19. valdrás
20. ¿tenéis?

21. ojalá que no traigas
22. vengo
23. es posible que tengan
24. no valgo
25. es imposible que hayas venido
26. no traería
27. tuvieron
28. trajeron
29. ¿vendrán?
30. era posible que tuviérais
31. si valiera
32. tenías
33. traigamos
34. ha tenido
35. has traído
36. ¿no tuvieron?
37. no valdría
38. estáis trayendo
39. era posible que viniéramos
40. era posible que trajera

19 IRREGULAR PAST PARTICIPLES

Aplicación

p. 129

1. that I will see
2. if they had discovered
3. if we saw
4. that you saw/have seen
5. you would see
6. we saw
7. we have described
8. that he will see

9. he will have died
10. you were seeing
11. you will see
12. I had resolved
13. we see
14. you saw
15. they would have returned

Mastery Test

pp. 129–130

1. no vemos
2. veían
3. si vierais (vieseis)
4. no había escrito
5. ojalá que veas
6. no vio
7. ¿han descubierto?
8. es posible que haya visto

9. veríamos
10. no ha cubierto
11. veía
12. no verá
13. es posible que haya visto
14. habrían abierto
15. ¿no veis?

Repaso de verbos irregulares

pp. 130–132

A.
1. he will have come
2. you had
3. they would go
4. you will say
5. you went (were)
6. he would want
7. we see
8. I was (went)
9. I brought
10. he was going out
11. you will have known
12. they might be
13. we had been able
14. I would have put
15. that they will give
16. that I will walk
17. if they fell
18. that we are worth
19. he had fitted
20. you heard
21. he will have satisfied
22. he would not do
23. we lead
24. you would seize
25. you used to translate
26. that there was/have been/were
27. she says
28. we go
29. we had been
30. you will have
31. they used to come
32. that they saw/have seen
33. you wanted
34. he used to bring
35. they gave
36. that you will be
37. you used to go out
38. you used to put
39. we can
40. we will know
41. we had heard
42. you will have been worth
43. that I did/have done
44. you will satisfy
45. I will fall
46. she walked
47. that he will fit
48. there will be
49. they translated
50. that I will drive

B.
1. ojalá que sea
2. habremos venido
3. decías
4. ¿va?
5. era imposible que viéramos
6. tuvieran (tuviesen)
7. habías querido
8. traería
9. es posible que sepa
10. estamos
11. habrás puesto
12. podía
13. no hemos dado
14. no salió
15. ojalá que no haya caído
16. oíamos
17. cayó
18. valdríamos
19. anduvo
20. cupe
21. no haré
22. traducían
23. habrían asido
24. condujo
25. es posible que deduzcas
26. habría
27. habrá dicho
28. iría
29. es posible que hayan visto
30. olajá que tengan
31. venía
32. quería
33. habéis sido
34. no traigamos
35. no sabe
36. pudiste
37. estaremos
38. ¡den!
39. saldría
40. pondréis
41. es posible que oiga
42. no andaremos
43. cabré
44. Ud. ha valido
45. si satisficiéramos (satisficiésemos)
46. no hicimos
47. caigo
48. es posible que asgamos
49. hubieran (hubiesen) sido
50. si condujera (condujese)

Repaso general 2

pp. 132–134

A.
1. we think
2. you opened
3. that they will lose
4. she answers
5. I understand
6. I arrived
7. you will say
8. he had fun
9. I sleep
10. we brought
11. I did
12. they will come
13. that you know/will know
14. if I put
15. that we are able/will be able
16. you may choose
17. if we returned
18. that they (will) take out
19. that they distinguish
20. if I looked for
21. I will read
22. you would know
23. they will have
24. I gave
25. you will see
26. he insinuates
27. that I (will) start
28. we send (sent)
29. that I (have) played
30. that I (will) trust

B.
1. escribíamos
2. entiende
3. viven
4. viajaban (estaban viajando)
5. guardas
6. traían (estaban trayendo)
7. ¿decimos?
8. quiere
9. se vistió
10. no vieron
11. salimos
12. si pusiera
13. no han hecho
14. no sé
15. pudiste
16. dirigimos
17. busqué
18. si escogerian/eligieran
19. ¡expliquen!
20. ojalá que llegue
21. vales
22. ¿leyeron?
23. si dieras
24. no vayamos
25. ojalá que tenga
26. es posible que jueguen
27. negué
28. ojalá que continúe
29. no empecé
30. es imposible que manden

Repaso general 3

pp. 134–135

A.
1. I began
2. that I (will) play
3. we were denying
4. she continues
5. they will send
6. you get
7. I had
8. you led
9. I was going out
10. they knew (found out)
11. he would hear
12. you fit
13. he may put
14. we would be able
15. I come
16. they will have died
17. I was laughing
18. he was contributing
19. he destroys
20. you used to possess
21. that they (will) build
22. he loses
23. we were serving
24. he used to know
25. she wounded
26. I may think
27. they threw
28. he will have lost
29. you were listening
30. she had returned

B.
1. jugabais
2. si empezaran
3. continúo
4. es posible que confíe
5. no leen
6. no quiso
7. serían
8. no corrijo
9. fui
10. dijo
11. es posible que vea
12. Ud. caía
13. hice
14. he puesto
15. saldrán
16. es posible que lea
17. habíamos dormido
18. si nos riéramos
19. es posible que muera
20. no creyeron
21. envie
22. ¿consentís?
23. ojalá que no destruyan
24. repetía
25. perdíamos
26. no vuelves (devuelves)
27. pasábamos
28. vivía
29. entendisteis
30. han abierto

20 FINAL REVIEW

Para practicar 1

p. 142

1. aprendo, aprendía, aprendí
2. zurce, zurcía, zurció
3. peca, pecaba, pecó
4. avergonzamos, avergonzábamos, avergonzamos
5. os erguís, os erguíais, os erguisteis
6. sollozas, sollozabas, sollozaste
7. se visten, se vestían, se vistieron
8. caben, cabían, cupieron
9. huele, olía, olió
10. yazgo, yacía, yací
11. expone, exponía, expuso
12. apaciguan, apaciguaban, apaciguaron
13. te gradúas, te graduabas, te graduaste
14. roo, roía, roí
15. se enoja, se enojaba, se enojó
16. poseemos, poseíamos, poseímos
17. almuerzas, almorzabas, almorzaste
18. revuelven, revolvían, revolvieron
19. huye, huía, huyó
20. salgo, salía, salí
21. desniegan, desnegaban, desnegaron
22. suponéis, suponíais, supusisteis
23. se levanta, se levantaba, se levantó
24. compadecemos, compadecíamos, compadecimos
25. ahogas, ahogabas, ahogaste

Para practicar 2

p. 143

A.
1. vamos
2. habéis estado
3. ellos arriesgarían
4. ellas habían querido
5. se divirtieron
6. os levantasteis
7. hubieran escuchado
8. estamos traduciendo
9. hayamos fregado
10. dormiríais

B.
1. hubiera avergonzado
2. habías tomado
3. habría hablado
4. habrá dormido
5. no haya desconfiado
6. he estado comiendo
7. había dicho
8. hubiese sentido
9. habré olido
10. hubieses vestido

Para practicar 3

pp. 143–144

A.
1. he estudiado
2. ha necesitado
3. hemos contado
4. habéis ofendido
5. han dicho
6. has sido
7. he molido
8. ha supuesto
9. han dormido
10. habéis descrito

B.
1. complacería
2. ofenderíais
3. dirías
4. sostendrían
5. se entrenaría
6. nos meceríamos
7. extinguiría
8. sabrían
9. venderían
10. ¿acertaría?

Para practicar 4

p. 144

A.
1. escuchando
2. careciendo
3. midiendo
4. estando
5. siendo
6. persiguiendo
7. advirtiendo
8. vistiéndose
9. sirviendo
10. huyendo

B.
1. abierto
2. ejercido
3. supuesto
4. revuelto
5. hecho
6. descubierto
7. agradecido
8. satisfecho
9. costado
10. vuelto

Para practicar 5

pp. 144–145

A.

sirve, influye, vive, decae, huele.

B.

reñí, sonreí, seguí, contraje, resolví.

C.

comprendáis, convengáis, encontréis, insinuéis, repitáis.

D.

habrá muerto, habrá perdido, habrá escrito, habrá propuesto, habrá cabido.

E.

oíamos, nos enriquecíamos, desconocíamos, negábamos, uníamos.

Para practicar 6

p. 145

rasques, asgas, friegues, tuerzas, cargues.

escuchemos, conduzcamos, descontinuemos, destruyamos, neguemos.

contraiga, crea, delinca, valga, conteste.

sequéis, gimáis, os habituéis, aborrezcáis, escondáis.

duerma, surja, impida, prepare, diga.

Aplicación 1

p. 146

1. that I (will) have
2. that Juan y Pedro (will) have fun/amuse themselves
3. you had gone out
4. they were consenting
5. I will have written
6. he would speak
7. you had revolved
8. they measured
9. I used to notice
10. that you felt
11. if you had moved
12. when will you begin?
13. come!
14. if you had had fun/amused yourself
15. she would have believed
16. you may not trust! (do not trust!)
17. are you going to play?
18. we will dry
19. I was cleaning
20. she needed
21. we would be able
22. you offended
23. you may find
24. Juan used to laugh
25. you had
26. we used to dress
27. he will have sobbed
28. he had
29. we were studying
30. we had not found
31. if we slept
32. that you (have) traveled
33. you would know
34. they need
35. that I measured/would measure

Aplicación 2

p. 147

1. dormimos (dormíamos)
2. influyeras (influyeses)
3. abrió (abría)
4. había revuelto
5. habíais elegido
6. rogaron (rogaban)
7. desconocisteis (desconocíais)
8. no bebiesen
9. fuimos (éramos)
10. pasamos (pasábamos)
11. encontramos (encontrábamos)
12. expusiera
13. se enriqueciesen
14. creímos (creíamos)
15. habíais aceptado
16. cargasen
17. fueron (eran)
18. distinguisteis (distinguíais)
19. habíamos convocado
20. compitieras
21. estaban corriendo
22. obedeciésemos
23. finjierais (finjieseis)
24. estuvieron (estaban)
25. aborrecimos (aborrecíamos)

Aplicación 3

pp. 147–148

1. estamos oliendo
2. vivimos
3. admirábamos
4. merecían
5. hayáis desaparecido
6. habrían ejercido
7. obliguéis
8. gemiréis
9. compusieran
10. aprenderíamos
11. riñeron
12. hayan conseguido
13. ¡corran!
14. habríamos pensado
15. huyáis
16. nos estamos habituando a
17. han
18. habéis colgado
19. hubierais desconfiado
20. no esparzáis
21. pecaremos
22. sonreísteis
23. hayan dormido
24. nos sentaríamos
25. habíais erguido

Aplicación 4

p. 148

1. haya hablado
2. habían comido
3. habíais estado
4. habrán pasado
5. no hubierais confiado
6. hayas extinguido
7. habremos movido
8. hayan molido
9. hayáis sentido
10. hayamos perseguido
11. habrás entrado
12. hubieses carecido
13. te habrás enriquecido
14. han ofrecido
15. habrías decaído
16. habrá sido
17. habríais colocado
18. había huido
19. he influido
20. hubieran acordado
21. habías aprobado
22. habrías asistido
23. habréis llegado
24. hubieseis delinquido
25. había reído

Aplicación 5

p. 149

1. necesitáramos (necesitásemos)
2. rogase
3. pagaras
4. preparaseis
5. pusiese
6. produjera
7. Pedro y Elena abriesen
8. apaciguara
9. impidiesen
10. mecieran
11. compadecieseis
12. prosiguieras
13. pagasen
14. complaciera
15. jugásemos
16. tuviera
17. colocase
18. apagaras
19. emprendiesemos
20. tomara
21. repitieseis
22. arriesgaran
23. enseñase
24. satisficiera
25. encogiese

Mastery Test 1

pp. 149–151

1. decidiré
2. estamos exigiendo
3. si hubieran asido
4. Juan y Pedro comieron
5. gastaríais
6. he mentido
7. ella escucha
8. estábamos viniendo
9. que leyeran (leyesen)
10. él ha recordado
11. no caeré
12. tuvimos
13. si hubiera pagado
14. ojalá que alcancemos
15. regreso
16. él tiene
17. él no habría rezado
18. es posible que haya visto
19. estábamos riñendo
20. dormías
21. él caminó
22. ¿esparció ella?
23. respondisteis
24. ¿estaba Ud. sirviendo?
25. ¿correrá ella?
26. sonreímos
27. es posible que Gil, Ana y Luis asgan
28. llevaban
29. no lo creo
30. habré molido
31. ojalá que no convenzan
32. está lloviendo (llueve)
33. ellos vendieron
34. Ud. volvió
35. ellos se habrían vestido

Mastery Test 2

p. 151

1. I will eat
2. if you played
3. I lie
4. we used to compete
5. he would conquer
6. you fit
7. she had convinced
8. they stumbled
9. you were preparing
10. that they (will) deny
11. I admire
12. I have eaten
13. they will speak
14. do not decide!
15. you might have talked
16. that I (will) maintain
17. we have said
18. you would have found
19. I washed
20. you were thinking
21. they didn't use to load
22. you had embarrassed
23. we will defy
24. I will have lit
25. you demand
26. she had supposed
27. you are lying
28. María and José will pay
29. you exercised
30. they dressed
31. we were biting
32. I would continue
33. you might indicate
34. you used to know
35. Don't stop!

Mastery Test 3

pp. 152–153

1. es posible que se haya lavado
2. me vestí
3. nos hemos divertido
4. ella se peinó el cabello
5. ellos se lavaban
6. Uds. se han levantado
7. si hubieran acordado
8. él se estaba lavando
9. me habituaré a
10. os lavasteis
11. si se hubiera enojado
12. ¡vistámonos!
13. me estoy acostando
14. ojalá que se laven
15. te habrías acordado
16. ella se está entrenando
17. él se había acostado
18. ellos se habrán esforzado
19. nos sentemos
20. ella se está enriqueciendo
21. Miguel se ha levantado
22. me irguiera
23. ellos se habituaron a
24. ella se divertía
25. me levantaré
26. ¡no os sentéis!
27. ellas se están vistiendo
28. si nos graduásemos
29. ¿estamos esforzándonos?
30. ojalá que se hayan lavado
31. ellos se acostarían
32. me divierto
33. María se peinaba el cabello
34. él se habría entrenado
35. nos enojamos

Mastery Test 4

pp. 153–154

1. haya tomado
2. hemos medido
3. habrás desconfiado
4. ha obedecido
5. se había acostado
6. habían ejercido
7. hubiese distinguido
8. hayas dispuesto
9. hayáis influido
10. habréis sollozado
11. haya acertado
12. hubiéramos expuesto
13. habrán elegido
14. habríamos hablado
15. me he acostado
16. has subido
17. habrán aborrecido
18. habríamos movido
19. hayamos cabido
20. habéis obedecido
21. hubiesen olido
22. había elegido
23. hubiéramos corregido
24. hubiese explicado
25. ha llovido

Repaso 1

p. 154

1. he will have come
2. you smelled
3. that you (will) say
4. Elena laughed
5. we are
6. I quarrel
7. you fitted
8. if we broke the law
9. that you (will) want
10. we are falling
11. they walked
12. he smells
13. we have conducted
14. you would have said
15. she used to wander
16. you might give
17. you deduced
18. that I (have) said
19. if they blessed
20. I would go
21. you will have done
22. they will satisfy
23. that we (will) go
24. you would not put
25. if you left

Repaso 2

pp. 154–155

1. acabamos
2. habláis
3. comisteis
4. habrían partido
5. estudiarán
6. comprendan
7. hemos preguntado
8. beberéis
9. escuchaban
10. abrimos
11. entrasteis
12. vivieron
13. hubieran tomado
14. temamos
15. habremos estudiado
16. ¿se habrán graduado?
17. estábamos llevando
18. escribirían
19. comprenderemos
20. entren
21. hayan leído
22. habíamos vendido
23. habéis trabajado
24. prepararían
25. nos hubiesen amado

Repaso 3

pp. 155–156

1. ojalá que entienda
2. si hubieras hablado
3. que dijéramos
4. es posible que no sonrías
5. si hubiera desaparecido
6. es posible que no desaparezca
7. es imposible que haya dormido
8. si advirtiérais
9. es posible que mintamos
10. si se peinara
11. es posible que haya desconfiado
12. ojalá que aprendan
13. si hubierais tropezado
14. que fuera
15. es posible que venda
16. es posible que Ana y Juan compitan
17. es posible que se vista
18. si hubiéramos necesitado
19. si se hubieran acostado
20. es posible que no hayan torcido
21. ojalá que se acuerde/recuerde
22. yo calentaría
23. es posible que hayamos enseñado
24. si siguiera
25. es posible que os hayáis levantado

Repaso 4

pp. 156–157

1. she prepares
2. are they entering?
3. we will have prevented
4. I arrived
5. you will have satisfied
6. they are mistrusting
7. we had composed
8. they would notice
9. he used to continue
10. I straighten up
11. bless us!
12. you will have analyzed
13. if we stopped
14. that he will conduct
15. you will sob
16. I would have fought
17. Elisa and Marta had thought
18. if we got
19. you would study
20. we will have been worth
21. that they would live
22. do not lie!
23. she may impose
24. that you had persecuted
25. you were showing
26. if they went to bed
27. she mended
28. you had embraced
29. she would want
30. it will snow
31. you may have descended
32. that we (will) live
33. he may not place
34. you used to be
35. that I (have) gnawed
36. you would have made
37. I compose
38. if we went
39. if you had left
40. that they would get

Repaso 5

pp. 157–158

1. iré
2. está lloviendo (llueve)
3. ojalá que duerma
4. habíamos lanzado
5. ellos estaban jugando
6. ella ha marcado
7. si Juan y Ana supieran
8. ella habrá ejercido
9. yo conduciría
10. ¡entra!
11. es imposible que dispongamos
12. ella no (se) merece
13. si hubieran descubierto/encontrado
14. no vayamos
15. ojalá que paren/detengan
16. él escucha
17. si laváramos
18. yo molestaría
19. María delinquirá
20. ella vale
21. estamos viajando
22. me estoy peinando el cabello
23. es posible que influyan
24. él había conquistado
25. ellos explicarían

Repaso 6

p. 158

A.
1. partimos
2. comíais
3. unían
4. habían salido
5. ¡acuéstense!
6. ¡no me pidáis!
7. corregiríamos
8. hayan confesado
9. se habrán acostado
10. discernieron
11. nos hubiésemos despertado
12. desapareceréis
13. bendecís
14. olamos
15. se peinaron

B.
1. marques
2. repitan
3. salgamos
4. quepa
5. consienta
6. expliquéis
7. aborrezcan
8. elija
9. hayan
10. hagan
11. vayan
12. irgamos
13. encojas
14. encuentre
15. complazca

Repaso 7

p. 159

A.

yerra, huye, cierra, gime, muere, niega, dispone, encuentra, prosigue, ha.

B.

contemos, revolvamos, castiguemos, surjamos, lavémonos, conduzcamos, parezcamos, saquemos, escondamos, santigüemos.

C.

coligiera (coligiese), mantuviese, cubriera, persiguiese, decayera, anduviese, acogiera, quisiese, durmiera, influyese.

Repaso 8

pp. 159–160

1. había acertado
2. hayan hablado
3. habrían hablado
4. habíamos dicho
5. hemos mantenido
6. habíais hecho
7. habían corrido
8. hubieras advertido
9. habré descubierto
10. habían colocado
11. hayan almorzado
12. se hubiese dispuesto
13. habéis adornado
14. me habré vestido
15. hubiéramos roído
16. habías abierto
17. he ofrecido
18. hubieran herido
19. hayáis fatigado
20. había sabido

Index of Infinitives, English to Spanish

O

obey   obedecer, 89
oblige   obligar, 81
obtain   conseguir, 86, 94
offend   ofender, 24
offer   ofrecer, 89
open   abrir, 6, 129

P

pacify   apaciguar, 82
pass   pasar, 18
pay   pagar, 80–81
persecute   perseguir, 86, 94
pity   compadecer, 89
place, put   colocar, 80; poner, 117
play   jugar, 93
please   complacer, 89
possess   poseer, 88
pray   rogar, 81, 93; rezar, 81
prepare   preparar, 18
pretend   fingir, 85
prevent   impedir, 77
produce   producir, 108
propose   proponer, 117
prosecute   proseguir, 86, 94
punish   castigar, 81
pursue   perseguir, 86, 94
put, place   poner, 117; colocar, 80

R

rain   llover, 70
read   leer, 6, 88
reach   alcanzar, 81
receive   recibir, 3, 6
recognize   reconocer, 89
reject   rechazar, 81
repeat   repetir, 77
reply   responder, 18; replicar, 80; contestar, 6
return   volver, 69, 129; devolver, 70, 129
revolve   revolver, 70, 129
risk   arriesgar, 81
run   correr, 18

S

satisfy   satisfacer, 113
say, tell   decir, 109
scatter   esparcir, 84
scratch   rascar, 80

see   ver, 128
seem   parecer, 89
seize   asir, 104; coger, 85
sell   vender, 2, 6
send   enviar, 89
serve   servir, 77
show   enseñar, 6; mostrar, 70
shrink   encoger, 85
sin   pecar, 80
sit   sentarse, 71
sleep   dormir, 73–74
smell   oler, 116–17
smile   sonreír, 95
snow   nevar, 70
sob   sollozar, 81
speak   hablar, 1, 8, 13, 20, 26, 31, 36–37, 42, 48, 51
spend   pasar, 18
spoil   consentir, 74
stir   revolver, 70, 129
stop   detener, 124
study   estudiar, 6
stumble   tropezar, 81, 94
succeed   acertar, 70; conseguir, 86, 94
suppose   suponer, 117
sustain   sostener, 124

T

take   tomar, 2, 6; coger, 85
take out   sacar, 80
teach   enseñar, 6
tell   contar, 69; decir, 109
thank   agradecer, 89
think   pensar, 69
threaten   amenazar, 81
throw   echar, 18; lanzar, 81
tire   fatigar, 81
translate   traducir, 108
travel   viajar, 18
trust   confiar, 89
try hard   esforzarse, 94
turn off   apagar, 81
turnover   revolver, 70, 129

U

understand   comprender, 15; entender, 69
undertake   emprender, 24
unite   unir, 6

Index of Spanish Infinitives